CLI

CLIFF RICHARD

Gale Barker

MarshallPickering
An Imprint of HarperCollins*Publishers*

Marshall Pickering is an imprint of
HarperCollins*Religious*
Part of HarperCollins*Publishers*
77-85 Fulham Palace Road, London W6 8JB

First published in Great Britain in 1991
by Marshall Pickering
3 5 7 9 10 8 6 4

A catalogue record for this book
is available from the British Library

ISBN 0 551 02149 7

Printed and bound in Great Britain by
HarperCollinsManufacturing, Glasgow

CONTENTS

1.

FROM A DISTANCE

It was Wembley, London, 17th June 1989, and over two evenings 140 thousand people of all ages and backgrounds had crowded into the massive stadium. In the darkness, you could hardly see their faces, but you could feel their excitement. It was a never-to-be-forgotten occasion, both for them and for the man they had come to watch, pop star Cliff Richard. This two and a half million pound extravaganza was his way of celebrating thirty dazzling years in show business.

Towards the end of the concert, Cliff stood alone on a high podium, shining in the spotlight against the unlit stadium. The show had been a great success – an exhilarating evening of old favourites and new hits, accompanied by energetic dance routines which proved he was as fit as ever, even though he was nearly fifty. Now he was still. A hush fell on the audience, as the mood changed and the star opened up his heart to his fans to thank them for supporting him over so many years.

"For thirty years you've given me a really glorious career. All I've been able to do in return really is just the best that I can do."

The audience went wild. Clearly they were more than happy with Cliff's best. He waited for them to finish, then spoke again, quietly, but with deep conviction. He was grateful for his career, for all his success, but there was something he really wanted to say, something important. Yes, he had spent thirty marvellous years in show business but, he said, "in this strange industry, what does it really all matter? If I have one thing to tell you that's of value, it's that God exists, that Jesus is alive."

The introductory bars sounded for the closing number, "From a Distance", an inspiring ballad, which underscored Cliff's words. It was one of his newer songs, but the message was one he had been singing throughout his life — of hope, of freedom, of justice, of harmony. It was a perfect ending to the concert. The audience was ecstatic, and Cliff's eyes filled with emotion as he acknowledged the applause of his fans, united with them in love and hope, and in memories of the past thirty years.

His life had been far more fulfilling than he could ever have envisaged. Who would have guessed that young Harry Webb from Cheshunt would turn into Cliff Richard, the world famous pop star? Who would have believed that, thirty years on, he would still be at the top of his profession? And who would have expected God to come into his life and turn it upside down?

When he was seven years old, young Harry Webb had no such fantastic dreams. Life was difficult enough without pondering the future; all he cared about was getting through each day. It had been a huge change, moving with his parents from their home in India to a new life in Britain, and he was finding it tough to be a newcomer in a distant land.

School was over for the day, and half a dozen of Harry's least favourite classmates were already huddled at the school gate, waiting for him to arrive. Brushing past them without any sign of acknowledgement, he turned into the chill, grey, English street and stared hard at the dirty pavement.

"Let's see your wigwam, Harry", cried one boy.

"Indibum. Harry Webb's an Indibum", chanted the others, as they danced along behind him, ululating like the Red Indians they had seen in the Saturday Westerns.

"Idiots," muttered Harry under his breath. "You'd think they'd never seen a sun tan before."

He strode on resolutely, his head bowed, his lips tightly pursed. He knew that life in England

3

would be very different, but he had never guessed how much he would miss India. The Webbs were supposed to be going back to their roots, to good old England, but Harry found nothing familiar and comforting in the British way of life. Even the food was bland! How he longed for the aromatic curries that the servants used to bring to school for his lunch! And for the hot Indian sun!

Suddenly one of the bigger boys lunged at Harry, who swung round, fists at the ready. He stared hard at the lad's icy blue eyes, but then he remembered the promise he made to his parents after last week's fight. They already had quite enough to worry about without him getting into trouble at school. With a stern glare, he turned back, and carried on walking. Disappointed at not being able to provoke a reaction, the bully slunk off with his mates, leaving Harry to trudge home with only his thoughts for company.

Not that he was really going home. No. Home, his real home, was thousands of miles away. Harry had been born on 14th October 1940 at Lucknow in India, where his father, Rodger, worked as an area manager for a catering firm called Kelners. He had spent his first seven years first in Lucknow and then in Howrah, near Calcutta. Harry's early childhood had been happy and carefree, growing up in India with his parents and two younger sisters, Jacqueline and Donella.

He sighed, remembering the day when everything changed. He had been out shopping with his mother when suddenly they were hemmed in by a crowd of jostling Indians, one of whom accosted Mrs Webb. ''Why don't you go home to your own country, White woman?'' he shouted. That was the worst moment in Harry's life, the moment when he knew that India could no longer be home for his family.

The Indian ''Home Rule'' riots had been escalating, and even in their comfortable dwelling the family could hear gunshots being fired. When the country was granted independence in 1947, it became apparent that it was no longer safe for White people to live there. The Webbs decided to set sail for their homeland, although Harry found this description amusing, as none of the family, not even his parents, had been born there. In fact, they had never even visited England before then.

Maybe we should have gone to Australia instead, Harry wondered, fastening his blazer in an attempt to keep out the autumn English chill. Sunny Australia. That wouldn't have been quite so different from India. A friend of the family who was planning on settling there had offered to pay their passage.

Instead, the Webbs plumped for England, the land of their forefathers. They set sail for Britain in the autumn of 1948 on the *SS Ranghi*, leaving behind the only life they had ever known for a new one in a strange land thousands of miles away. Harry was violently sick for much of the three-week voyage, but eventually he found his sea legs. After what seemed like an eternity, the ship docked at Portsmouth and the Webbs took their first shaky steps on English soil, with only five pounds to their name.

Harry kicked aside a pile of soggy leaves and remembered how astonished he had been to see so many trees in his new homeland. They were everywhere – even at the railway stations. He had never seen so many trees in all his life. Lots of branches to get your kite strings caught in, he thought.

Kite flying. That was something else he missed. Back in India there was nothing Harry had enjoyed more than manoeuvring the diamond-shaped Indian kites, which were made out of tissue paper and bamboo and had character-istically short tails. Kite-flying was a highly competitive pastime, as the owners would rub their kite strings with a paste of ground glass and egg white in the hope of cutting their opponents' strings. Harry had got this trick down to a fine art, but what did it matter?

The memory of past kite-flying victories brought a smile to Harry's lips as he trudged home.

Perhaps he could fly a kite here in England? He'd show these English kids a thing or two!

But there would be no kite-flying for Harry tonight. Just a lonely walk back to Grandma's house in Carshalton in Surrey, where he and his two sisters huddled together with their parents in only one room. Not that Grandma was in any way to blame for their problems. On the contrary, she had been very generous towards them, and if it hadn't been for her, heaven only knows where they would have lived, given that Dad was finding it so difficult to find a steady job.

Maybe Dad would have had more luck with his job-hunting today? Harry hoped so. He knew how demoralising it was for his father to be unemployed, when he had been used to a responsible job in India, as an area manager for a catering firm. A proud and fiercely independent man, Rodger Webb hated not being able to provide for his family, but jobs were scarce in post-war Britain.

But in many ways it was Mum who had the most to cope with. Her new conditions were a particular shock to her after her privileged, cushioned lifestyle in India. There she always had servants to cook or clean for her, and she never had cause to worry about money. But in Britain she had to look after all the family within the confines of a single room at Grandma's house.

Two adults and three children squashed together, with no hope of a home of their own. Was it any wonder poor Mum cried herself to sleep at night?

Harry sighed at the thought of his mother's unhappiness. It seemed that there was just no room for the Webbs in this distant land – no home, no job, no friends. For a moment, he felt a lump in his throat, but he straightened the satchel on his back and gave himself a good talking to. He told himself there was no point in him feeling sorry for himself; they'd get over their problems eventually. ''They can laugh all they like,'' he resolved, ''I'll show them. Just you wait, one day they'll all want to know me, wigwam or no wigwam.''

Months passed and as Harry became integrated into the class and accepted by his classmates, those lonely walks home to Grandma's became a distant memory. His swarthy skin began to fade to a pinker tone in his new country's more temperate climate, and he soon picked up the London accent of his new school friends.

Then just as he was settling into his new school and his new area, the Webb family uprooted itself and he had to start all over again. Harry's father had been offered a job at Enfield, so the Webbs decided to move to nearby Waltham Cross. Rodger Webb was to work at Atlas Lamps, which was part of Ferguson's radio and television complex. It made sense to live nearer his place of work, and they might be able to find better accommodation in that area too.

But to begin with they were still obliged to lodge with another relative, this time an Aunt. Staying there was no improvement upon life at Grandma's, as the five of them still lived in one room. They slept in it and ate in it. They cooked in it and washed in it. Their plight became even more desperate when Harry's youngest sister, Joan, was born, bringing the number to six.

You can imagine how stressful it must have been to spend every day in such overcrowded conditions. Petty irritations blew up into full-scale rows, just because there was no space and no privacy. Their tension was exacerbated by the fact that there was no hope of getting a place of their own in the near future. Harry's mum and dad had their names down for a council house, but because of the length of the waiting list, it would be several years before their turn came to be rehoused.

However, the Webbs were to get their longed-for house sooner than they expected. A kind neighbour got a friend from the council to come and see the dreadful conditions in which they were living. He was appalled at their plight and promised to find them a council house. They still had to wait another twelve months before they got it, but eventually the day dawned when they were to move into a place of their own.

The Webbs were allocated a red-brick "three up and two down" on a council estate in Cheshunt. Now they had plenty of space, but the problem was they had nothing to put in it. There was no way they could afford to rush out and buy furniture for the whole house. At first they had to sleep on the floor as they didn't have any beds or mattresses. Mr Webb made a couple of armchairs out of old packing cases which he bought from his firm.

Fortunately they had always been a close-knit family. This gave Harry and his sisters a sense of security which compensated for any material things that they may have lacked. They all pulled together as best they could.

As soon as Joan was old enough to be left, Mrs Webb got a job doing the evening shift at a paintbrush factory. Harry was now eleven, and, as the eldest, he had the responsibility of looking after his sisters. He would get their tea ready and look after them until his dad came home. He would even prepare the baby's bottle and change her nappy.

Not long after they moved to their own house, Harry had a bitter disappointment to come to terms with. In those days all primary school children had to sit an examination at the age of eleven, "the eleven-plus", to determine which sort of secondary school they would go to. Those who were academically bright would be awarded places at a grammar school; the technically able could go to a technical school; and the rest went to a secondary modern.

At the King's Road School in Waltham Cross, Harry had won a prize for being the school's top boy in class work. He desperately wanted to go to grammar school and expected to win a place, but when the results came out, he was devastated to discover that he had not done well enough.

Failing to get to grammar school was bad enough, but Harry was mortified to find that he wasn't even in the top stream at his new school, Cheshunt Secondary Modern. However, he did manage to be transferred into it halfway through the first term, and once he had got over his initial disappointment, he was happy at that school, where there were plenty of opportunities for him to excel.

One of these was in sport. Harry was good at most sports, and set a school record for the javelin, but he was particularly good at football, gaining a place in the Hertfordshire schoolboys' county side. Indeed, he could have taken up football professionally, had he not been drawn towards a singing career.

At the age of fourteen Harry played Ratty in the

school production of *Toad of Toad Hall*, and had to sing a couple of songs. Quite a number of people complimented him on his singing, including his English teacher, Mrs Norris, who asked him if he'd thought of taking it up.

In fact, Harry was passionate about music. Even at that age he had made up his mind that he would be a pop singer. He spent hours listening to pop records and trying to look and sound like his hero, Elvis Presley. At the time, rock'n'roll was all the rage, and Elvis was one of the biggest stars. He was American, like most of the great rock'n'roll singers – Britain had not yet produced a singer to match them. The growth of this type of music had resulted in a new group of people – teenagers – with their own identity.

Until the late nineteen fifties, all the records, magazines, fashions and films that were produced were aimed at either adults or children, and there was nothing specifically for adolescents. But now teenagers were beginning to see themselves as a distinct category with their own special music, clothes, and entertainment. Instead of waltzing sedately to their parents' dance music, they wanted to jive to rock'n'roll, and their clothes – dirndl skirts and tight jumpers for the girls, drainpipe trousers and winkle-picker shoes for the boys – reflected their desire to break away from their parents' expectations.

One of the teenagers' preoccupations was rock'n'roll. Listening to this music was their way of rebelling against their parents and other people in authority, including the Church. With its primitive beat, it was exciting, and, above all, it was their own.

Needless to say, some parents were deeply suspicious of it. Some American critics had branded Elvis as ''obscene'' because of the way he swivelled his hips. The older generation said he was a bad influence on young people, and accused him of inciting them to riot. One pastor even held a meeting to pray for Elvis's salvation.

Harry's admiration for another rock'n'roll star, Bill Haley, got him into trouble at school. In 1957 Bill, an American, was touring Britain with his group, the Comets. They were putting on a show in Edmonton, just a couple of miles away from Harry's home. He and some of his friends, all of them prefects, decided to skip school to queue for tickets to the show.

The boys were found out, and the next morning they were dragged before the head and stripped of their prefects' badges. Harry protested at the injustice of this treatment: ''If we'd been to see the Bolshoi Ballet you'd have given us a pat on the back.''

His English teacher Mrs Norris tried to put the incident in perspective. ''I bet you in ten years' time you won't even remember the name, 'Bill Haley'.''

"Bet you I will," retorted Harry. "I bet you a box of chocolates that I will." Harry was right, and ten years later he went back to school to claim his chocolates.

With his talent for singing and his love for pop music, it was natural that Harry would want to sing in a group. The first one that he belonged to was the Quintones. Made up of three girls and two boys, it played at school concerts and Youth Fellowship dances at Cheshunt. The group sang unaccompanied and Harry used to provide an occasional solo.

His second group, the Dick Teague Skiffle Group, was slightly more serious. By this time Harry had left school and was working as a Credit Control Clerk at Atlas Lamps for four pounds and fifteen shillings a week (£4.75), in the same office as his father, but he knew that he really wanted to be a rock star. The skiffle group was his next step up the ladder.

Skiffle players used old washboards and home-made double basses for their do-it-yourself type of music. It was a national craze at the time, but Harry was not really keen on it. However, he reckoned that it would be good experience for him to sing regularly with an established group. He was encouraged to join by a friend of his, another rock'n'roller called Terry Smart, who already played for the group.

The group wanted Harry to play guitar, but at that time he didn't even own such a thing, let alone know how to play it. Fortunately his dad was able to teach him the basics using an old guitar of Terry's.

Although the band gave Harry a lot of experience playing regularly at weddings, parties and badminton club suppers, it didn't satisfy him. Rock'n'roll was still his real love. It wasn't long before he and Terry left and, with a school friend of Harry's, they formed their own rock group, the Drifters. Together with the third member, Norman Mitham, they used to practise together every night in the Webbs' council house.

Unfortunately, the building was not very well soundproofed, and in an attempt to get some peace, the neighbours complained to the housing authority. The official who came to investigate could have put paid to the lads' practice sessions, but he was remarkably lenient. The Drifters were allowed to continue their rehearsals, provided that they stopped by ten o'clock and kept all the doors and windows shut.

Although they were doing quite well in their own small world, playing at dances and youth events, Harry was still an ordinary young lad from a council estate, who worked in a factory, and sang in a group in his spare time. But soon everything would change dramatically. Before long, young Harry Webb from Atlas Lamps would have a new life as an international star, and a new name – Cliff Richard.

2.

ENTER CLIFF RICHARD

A familiar voice roused Harry from his daydreams. "Interesting view out there, son?"

Harry looked up at his father's reproachful face, and flushed with guilt. He realised that he must have been staring out of the window for the past five minutes.

"Mmn . . . Oh, sorry, Dad. I was somewhere else . . ."

"I know you were, lad. In the dance hall or at a youth club concert, no doubt. But you're paid to be here, mind and body, so you'd better knuckle down to it or you'll be in trouble with the boss."

Harry knew his dad was right. His mind wasn't on his job at all. He just wasn't able to concentrate on his job and give it his full attention. He knew he wasn't doing as well as he ought to, and he felt especially bad about it because his father worked in the same office and could see that he wasn't settling into his work.

But then Harry didn't find it easy being a Credit

Control Clerk at Atlas Lamps. Sitting all day at a desk in a big open-plan office, sorting out the accounts into regions was not the ideal way to spend your days. Not if you had no idea of geography and no interest in business. Not if all you cared about was rock'n'roll. Not if you lived only for those precious hours when you could make music.

"I'll try, Dad. Don't you worry," he promised, seeing the anxiety in his father's eyes.

Rodger smiled, and went back to his own desk. He knew that Harry wasn't a bad lad. And he was bright enough. If only he'd settle down instead of messing around playing that rock'n'roll music . . .

Harry tried to focus his attention on the huge pile of invoices that littered his desk, but everything felt wrong. This wasn't where he belonged. If only he could spend all his time on his music . . .

But Harry knew there was no way he could give up his day job at the moment. The band were playing lots of gigs, but they only earned peanuts. No, he would just have to stay at Atlas Lamps. At least it helped to think about the next gig, to dream about the day when music would be his career as well as his passion.

What did they matter, all these accounts? They were nothing to get excited about, just bits of paper.

Tonight though, that was a different matter. Tonight the Drifters had an engagement at the Five Horseshoes. Who could say what might happen there?

Playing at the Five Horseshoes in Hoddesdon was considered to be a step up from the youth clubs and Saturday night dances that were the Drifters' usual haunts. The Drifters played with all the verve that this new venue merited, but the reaction they got from the audience was much the same as usual. However one young man came over and spoke to them at the end of the performance. He was barely older than Harry.

"Excuse me," he said, "I really enjoyed your music. Do you have a manager?"

A manager? Was this some sort of a joke? After all, they were only a bunch of lads who played at local hops in their spare time. Harry nearly burst out laughing at the very idea. Instead, he murmured, "No, not yet."

"In that case, will you let me manage your band?" asked the young man.

The Drifters' strange admirer either had remarkable foresight or else he was completely mad. Imagine thinking they needed a manager! Still, what did they have to lose?

"You're on." They shook hands on it. And that was the start of a very important relationship. The Drifters were to owe a lot to that young man from the Five Horseshoes – Johnny Foster.

In terms of show business experience Johnny Foster was just as green as the Drifters. He spent his days in the sewage works, a far cry from the glamour and glitz of the recording studios which the group aspired to. But Johnny was exactly what they needed. He was someone who believed in going out and making things happen.

One of his first schemes was to borrow money from his parents so that the Drifters could pay to make a private recording at the HMV store in Oxford Street. It cost five pounds – a fortune in those days, if you consider that Cliff was by then only earning four pounds and fifteen shillings a week at Atlas Lamps. Nowadays nearly everyone has a cassette recorder at home, but at that time musicians had to pay if they wanted a sample of their work to give to agents and record companies. The Drifters' record was played to Tommy Steele's agent, Ian Bevan, but he was not impressed, and advised Harry not to give up his day job.

John Foster was undeterred by this criticism. He was full of grand schemes for the group. His next brainwave was to fix up the Drifters to spend a week at the 2i's in Soho.

Today Soho is full of sex shops and cinemas showing soft porn movies. But in the fifties it was very different. It was a cosmopolitan area of

London, whose coffee shops, or espresso bars as they were called, were very popular with young people. They gathered there to listen to live music as well as to drink coffee.

Of all these coffee bars, the most exciting was a plain little place called the 2i's, so named because the first owners were two brothers called Irani. The next owners, a couple of all-in wrestlers, wanted to provide a showcase for young performers, and the café attracted such famous talent scouts as Lionel Bart (who was to write the music for the show *Oliver*). Tommy Steele and Terry Dene had both been discovered there.

The Drifters went each night to the 2i's, full of hope that tonight would be the night when someone would recognise their talent and set on the path to stardom. But it was not to be. That week there was no one important there to spot them, and there wasn't much left from their ten shilling (50p) fee once they'd paid for their taxi home.

But John Foster had other tricks up his sleeve. He'd heard that a talent contest was to be held at the Gaumont in Shepherd's Bush. The band had already tried to take part in another talent contest but had been forced to withdraw shame-faced when they couldn't get their amplifier to work. Instead of letting the Drifters take their chances as contestants, John Foster shrewdly offered to have them play at the end of the show without payment.

The management jumped at this money-saving offer, but the Drifters weren't really losing out. The experience they would gain was more valuable than any money. It was a rare opportunity to play to a packed house. The boys had never had such a terrific audience reaction as they did that night. Everyone screamed and applauded so much that Harry could hardly believe it was all happening.

"So this is what it's like to be successful," he thought as he took his bow before row upon row of enthusiastic teenagers. "I could get used to this."

The Drifters were invited back to the 2i's for another booking, and this time someone did notice them. He was a promoter called Bob Greatorex, and he booked the group to appear at a ballroom in Derbyshire. There was only one problem – he didn't like the name Harry Webb and the Drifters.

"Can't you think of something more exciting?" he asked the lads over a drink at a nearby pub. "Something that will look good on the bill boards."

"All right. How about Russ Clifford?"

Harry wasn't sure. Russ was a very soft name. "I think we need something with more bite."

They thought of Cliff Russard, but they didn't really like Russard, and changed it to Richards. Then Ian Samwell had a brainwave.

"Not Richards. Leave off the 's' and make it just 'Cliff Richard'. People will get it wrong and we can correct them. That way the name will be mentioned twice, and people will take more notice of it."

Harry Webb was now Cliff Richard. He still used his old name at work in the office, but at home he was Cliff. His family tried their best to get used to his new name, but occasionally they faltered.

"Could you pass the cornflakes, Harry? Whoops, Cliff!" blushed Donna. "Sorry . . . Cliff."

A month after their appearance at the talent show in Shepherd's Bush, they played again at the Gaumont, again for no payment, but this time John Foster had worked his magic and persuaded a well-known agent called George Ganjou to come and watch them. Again the group made a tremendous impression on the thousand or so youngsters who'd come to watch. But it was George Ganjou's opinion that counted.

"Did you like the act?" Cliff asked him after the show.

"It was quite good," conceded George, without much enthusiasm. Cliff's heart sank. He couldn't understand it. The audience had loved them, so why didn't George Ganjou? In fact, George was not a devotee of rock'n'roll, but nevertheless he could see that the group had promise.

"I'll tell you what," said George, "if you make a recording, I'll play it to my friend, Norrie Paramor."

Norrie Paramor! He was a recording manager at EMI. Thank goodness John had already got them to make a demo disc. They gave it to George and waited nervously for Norrie Paramor's verdict.

In fact, Norrie was more impressed by another tape which he had received from an opera singer. Nevertheless, he agreed to give the Drifters an audition when he got back from holiday in two weeks' time. Those two weeks were the longest the boys had ever known. They were so excited they could hardly stop thinking about record contracts and tours and fame. But in between their fantasies, doubts crept in and they'd start to wonder, "What if he doesn't like us? What if nothing comes of it?" By the time they arrived for their audition at EMI's Studio 2 in Abbey Road, St John's Wood, they were sick with nerves.

Somehow they managed to calm themselves enough to play their pieces to him.

"Very good, very good," was Norrie Paramor's

reaction. "I think I've got just the song for you to record."

"Great! When do you want us?" Cliff replied.

Norrie hesitated. "Actually, Cliff, I was thinking of just you. I'm not so sure about the boys."

But Cliff managed to talk Norrie into using the Drifters on the record as well. The "A" side was to be a song called "Schoolboy Crush", with one of Ian Samwell's compositions, "Move It", on the back. The record was to be released on 29th August 1958, but meanwhile George Ganjou was busy fixing up other work for Cliff. He arranged for Cliff to work for four weeks at Butlin's Holiday Camp in Clacton at thirty pounds a week. But the Drifters were not included in the offer.

"If they don't go, neither do I," insisted Cliff, suggesting that he take a smaller fee so that the boys could go too. In the end the Drifters were also hired for nine pounds a week each, plus free board and lodgings.

For Cliff, this assignment inevitably meant the end of his career as a clerk. There was no way he could continue with his day job now. At last he could hand in his notice at Atlas Lamps and do what he really wanted. No more pieces of paper, no more sitting at a desk, no more long boring days in the office. Atlas Lamps wished him well and agreed he had never really been cut out for office life.

A couple of weeks later, Cliff signed a long-term contract. He was now a professional singer. But he would soon discover that life in show business isn't nearly as glamorous as people think it is. Before their stint at Butlin's, the Drifters were committed to a gig in Derbyshire which Bob Greatorex had arranged for them. That night the boys had to sleep on benches in the dance hall because they couldn't afford a hotel.

That minor discomfort was soon forgotten amidst the excitement of Butlin's. Yet even that had its own irritations. Butlin's didn't regard the Drifters as being unique, and wanted the boys to wear the same outfits as the other redcoats, the staff who were involved in entertainment. Johnny exercised his customary flair for getting attention and insisted that they be allowed to wear something a bit different. He succeeded, and instead of red jackets, the boys sported white shirts with a large red ''V'' motif on the front.

At the holiday camp, the band had a couple of false starts, as they were first instructed to play in the camp night-club, which was called the Calypso Room, and the pub, the Pig and Whistle, before they were eventually assigned to a more suitable venue – the Rock'n'Roll Ballroom.

''At last,'' Cliff breathed a sigh of relief as the boys took up their positions. ''Thank goodness it eventually dawned on them that this is where we should be. All those broken beer mugs and fights were really getting me down.''

Now the group could relax and enjoy playing for people who really wanted to hear their type of music. To do what they loved to do in a fun environment, and get paid for it, to boot, was a great treat, and one which they regarded with wonder.

''Pinch me, Cliff,'' said Ian Samwell, ''I swear that one of these days we'll wake up and find that this is all a dream.''

But there were even more exciting opportunities ahead for Cliff and his band. One of these was a fortnight's tour of Britain in October in a variety show, which was headed by an American duo, the Kalin Twins. The Drifters were to receive the stupendous fee of two hundred pounds for appearing. They were thrilled at this big opportunity, but they quickly realised that they would need reinforcements if they were to play at concerts of that magnitude. Their instrumental sound just wasn't big enough. At this point two very significant people stepped into Cliff's life.

One of them was a tall young man with glasses, who played the guitar like a virtuoso and looked like Buddy Holly. Johnny Foster had heard him perform at the 2i's and was hugely impressed.

''You're just the guy we're looking for,'' he said

after the music ended. "How do you fancy coming on tour with the Drifters?"

"Sure," said the guitarist, Hank Marvin. "I'll come – but only on condition that you use my mate, as well."

"Who's he?" asked Johnny, intrigued.

"He's another guitarist – Bruce Welch."

But there was another milestone for Cliff even before the Kalin Twins tour. The group had already auditioned unsuccessfully for a television show called the *Six-Five Special*, a forerunner of *Top of the Pops*. But a producer called Jack Good, from the rival channel was very impressed by the "B" side of Cliff's record, Move It and asked Cliff to appear on the Independent Television pop programme, *Oh Boy!*

"Just one thing, Cliff," said Jack, as he watched the television rehearsals. "Stop trying to be Elvis. But you can keep the smoulder."

On Jack Good's instructions, Cliff shaved his Elvis side-burns and got rid of his guitar. He felt naked without it to hide behind, in spite of his long pink jacket, black shirt and trousers, and grey suede shoes, which were part of his "mean" look. Jack Good was a master of how to project an image on stage and television, and he taught Cliff how to hold his head, what to do with his arms, and how to angle his shoulders for maximum impact.

Cliff's first appearance on *Oh Boy!* aroused very little response from the public, but all of a sudden his career moved into another gear. "Move It" made the charts, and the next time he appeared on the show, Cliff was besieged by screaming fans.

It was the same story on the Kalin Twins Tour. At the start of the tour, the Kalin Twins were at number one in the hit parade with their record, "When?", and Cliff and the Drifters were just supporting artists. But in the middle of the tour, "Move It" reached number two in the charts and the Americans dropped to number nine.

Every night when the Kalin Twins tried to start their act, they were shouted down with cries of "We Want Cliff". To spare the American duo further embarrassment, the management tried to persuade the Drifters to change their place in the line-up, but the English boys stuck firmly to what was in their contract. The nightly commotion was the best publicity the Drifters could have hoped for.

3.

THE FLIP SIDE OF FAME

Cliff put down the newspaper in disgust. "I don't believe it, Mum. Where do they get it all from?"

"What is it now?" asked Mrs. Webb.

"It's about my appearance on *Oh Boy!* They're calling it 'crude exhibitionism'." He looked at his mother for reassurance. "My act isn't that bad, is it?"

"No, I don't think it's very shocking, Cliff. But then I know you, don't I?"

Moving into the limelight had brought a host of unforeseen problems for Cliff. In December 1958, there was much more of a generation gap than there is now, and many parents disapproved of this new phenomenon called rock'n'roll. Cliff's sultry pouts and provocative hip-swinging were reckoned to have sexual overtones, and were frowned upon by adults, concerned about the morality of their offspring. Their anxiety was fuelled by the press, who milked this new boy bombshell for every ounce of sensationalism they could get.

The *New Musical Express* called Cliff's hip-swinging "revolting", and wrote that his act was "hardly the kind of performance any parent could wish his children to witness". The *Daily Mirror* ran the headline, "Is this boy too sexy for television?", while another paper asked, "Is he a bad influence on your daughter?"

In interviews, Cliff tried to defend himself against the accusations of indecency. "I don't set out to be sexy," he insisted. "If people want to find me sexy they will." He always maintained in the face of press insinuations that his stage act was not intended to be vulgar. But in those days, Cliff's music and act were considered revolutionary. People were not used to seeing his sort of clothes and movements on television, and at the time there were only a few famous rock performers, like Tommy Steele, and Marty Wilde (Kim Wilde's father), so Cliff was subjected to the full glare of media attention.

But soon it wasn't just the verbal attacks of the press that were bothering him. That winter his shows became the target for physical disruption from a number of London gangs who had taken a dislike to the young star. Each time Cliff went on stage he knew that there could be between fifty and a hundred youths in the audience who had come for the sole purpose of causing trouble. At the Trocadero a guitar was damaged by something thrown on stage from the audience, then shortly after that at the Lyceum a concert degenerated into chaos when missiles were thrown and fights broke out between warring gangs of youths. The situation became so serious that Cliff and the Drifters had to be taken off stage halfway though their first song.

Cliff's work schedule had got out of hand as well. After turning professional, he made John Foster his personal road manager, and took on Franklyn Boyd as his professional manager. However, Boyd allowed the young star to take on far more commitments than he could reasonably handle. One week Cliff found himself getting up at five in the morning to work on the film *Serious Charge*, making records, appearing on two television shows, and doing two shows every night at the Finsbury Park Empire.

As you can imagine, all this was too much for eighteen-year-old Cliff to cope with, especially when it was combined with the emotional stress of bad publicity and gang disruptions. By the end of the week Cliff was physically shattered. He lost his voice and only got through his last stage performance by miming. When it was over he went home and slept so soundly that he didn't even hear his alarm go off the next morning. His mother, Dorothy, came to wake him in time for his rehearsal, and to her consternation, Cliff pleaded with her not to make him go to the film set.

"I can't do it, Mum. It's just too much for me. I almost wish I were back at Atlas Lamps. At least I wouldn't feel such a clapped-out old wreck."

Fortunately Rodger Webb stepped in and took a firm stand. "Don't you worry, lad. Just you get some sleep. I'll take care of everything."

He did. Mr Webb realised that Franklin Boyd had not been discriminating enough in planning Cliff's schedule, and had been too eager to say "yes" to offers of work. It was one thing to see that Cliff had enough to do, but surely there was no need to drive the poor boy into the ground? Just before Christmas, he wrote to Franklyn Boyd and told him that his contract as Cliff's manager was ended.

On Norrie Paramor's recommendation, Tito Burns was chosen as Cliff's new manager. Tito, who had been the leader of a popular band, signed a contract with Rodger Webb to manage Cliff until his twenty-first birthday. It may come as a shock for us to realise that, in spite of Cliff's achievements, he was still under twenty-one and so he was not legally able to sign his own contracts. Instead, his father had to sign all legal documents on his behalf.

The year 1958 had brought fame for Cliff, but it was fame at a price. December had not given him peace and good cheer, yet there was a glint of gold in and amongst all the turmoil. The *Daily Mirror* disc page named Cliff "New Boy of the Year". The accolade was a good omen for the coming year's work.

The film that Cliff was working on that winter, *Serious Charge*, was to change his whole career, because of one simple song, "Living Doll". When he sang it in the film, Cliff didn't like it very much, but later he and the Drifters included it on a record, where they played it at a slower, much more satisfactory pace. The bouncy ditty occupied the number one position in the charts for six weeks, and won a gold disc. More significantly, it lost Cliff his bad boy image and changed him from just a rock'n'roll singer, into an entertainer who appealed to all the family. Youngsters began to bring their parents along to see this singer, who now was less smouldering, less like his hero Elvis.

An invitation to appear at a mini Royal Command Performance set the monarchical seal of approval on Cliff's new image. Appearing with great names such as Tommy Trinder, Arthur Askey, and the Hallé Orchestra, Cliff was now, without any doubt, a respectable performer.

The year 1960 gave Cliff the chance to fulfil another long-standing ambition – to tour America. He and the Drifters, now renamed the Shadows to avoid confusion with an American group of the same name, were going to tour America and Canada for six weeks in a show that was billed as "The Biggest Show of Stars for 1960". Cliff was a supporting artist in a cast of American stars, led by Frankie Avalon. The shows were very successful, but personally, because of the gruelling schedule, Cliff saw very little of the country, and professionally the tour brought him very little benefit. This was probably because the record companies hadn't taken the trouble to liaise with the tour promoters.

Fame did not immediately bring Cliff the riches we associate with pop stars. He bought a television set with the first cheque he earned, and later followed it with a car, but until a year or so later, when record royalties began to come in, the Webbs were still living in their council house. Once the family had the means to buy something better, they moved to a semi-detached house six miles away, and decked it out with fitted carpets and the sort of furniture they had never been able to afford. A huge fence around the garden was a necessity, to keep Cliff's fans at bay.

Another of Cliff's films, *The Young Ones*, consolidated Cliff's new identity. This was a musical, in which he starred with the Shadows. A family film, it told the story of a group of youngsters who put on a show to save their youth club. It was a great box-office success, and Cliff was now a family favourite. It was followed by *Summer Holiday*, in which Cliff and some friends go off on holiday in a converted bus, another film which did very well. Unfortunately, Cliff's next film, *Wonderful Life*, was not such a pleasure to work on, as the production was beset by financial problems and bad weather, and fell badly behind schedule.

A lot had happened to the fledgling star Cliff in a very short space of time. In two or three years he had changed from a pale copy of Elvis, with a pink jacket and fluorescent socks, into a well-dressed, well-liked young man. Spurred on to diet after hearing a *Coronation Street* character call him ''a lovely chubby lad'', he had shed two and a half stone of puppy fat, and time had cured him of his teenage acne. Most importantly, he was no longer branded by the press as a crude exhibitionist. He was firmly established in the mind of the public as an inoffensive, all-round family entertainer. Yes, lots of changes had happened externally, but the next few years were to bring about equally important inner changes.

At the beginning of February 1961 Cliff and his manager, Tito Burns, separated, leaving Cliff, who was still a minor, under the guidance of his father. During the previous year, Mr Webb had been in and out of hospital and, because of this, Cliff had cancelled some engagements to be with him and help the family. Cliff was glad to do what he could for his father and enjoyed sharing in the family chores. However, his father did not cope so well with the changes which his illness imposed upon the family regime. He had always prided himself on his self-reliance and hated having to sit back and watch others do jobs which he had always done.

But he had no choice. Rodger Webb was very sick, and within three months he would die of heart disease. How would young Cliff cope without this strong, fiercely independent man, who had advised and encouraged and protected him for so long? What would his grief do to him?

4.

LOOKING FOR AN ANSWER

For nearly twenty-five years Cliff has spoken publicly and vociferously about his deeply-held Christian convictions. This makes it all the more astonishing to discover that when he first rose to stardom he had no interest in religion.

As a child in India, Cliff had belonged to a church choir; then when the family moved to Britain he used to go to church with his mother. That stopped when Mrs Webb got her job in the factory, as Sunday was then the only day when the family could be together.

Later, when he grew up and became involved with rock'n'roll, religion was relegated to the bottom of his list of priorities. Occasionally he would pray for a record to reach the top of the charts, but beyond that, God had no role to play in his life. It would be unfair to say that Cliff was an atheist, as he believed in the existence of a God of some sort. However, he took the view that it didn't matter whether someone was a Christian or a Muslim or a Buddhist, as long as he lived a decent life. He had no idea of what God might be like, and he couldn't be bothered to find out. Religion was irrelevant to him.

So how did Cliff become one of the most famous Christians of the twentieth century? How did God take centre-stage in his life, and become more important to him than even his much-loved career?

A dramatic conversion, like that of St Paul on the Damascus Road, might have been in keeping with Cliff's sensational show-business career. But the truth is that Cliff came to faith in Jesus Christ only after years of searching for an answer to the question, ''Surely there must be more to life than this?''

When fame and fortune seem far beyond our reach, it is easy to believe that they automatically bring happiness and contentment. Most of us never have the chance to discover that, even when our most precious dreams have come true, we may still feel unfulfilled.

By the age of twenty-one Cliff had already achieved more than most people could hope for in a lifetime, yet deep inside he felt that there was something missing from his life. He had everything he could possibly want – a hugely successful career, friends, a loving family, a magnificent home.

But in spite of all this, Cliff sensed that he lacked

something. "I don't know what it is that's wrong with me," he told himself, "I just feel there must be something more to life. There must be." Even Cliff himself cannot really identify what it was that triggered off this inner yearning, but he has suggested that his father's death may have had a deep subconscious effect on him.

Cliff's father had been ill for about six months with heart trouble, as a result of which he had already had one spell in hospital. A fiercely independent man, he hated being unable to fulfil his share of the family responsibilities, although Cliff was quite happy to mend fuses and mow the lawn. Although the family were aware of the gravity of Mr Webb's illness, they had pushed their deepest fears to the back of their minds. There was a period of two or three months when he appeared to be getting better, so, perhaps he would recover from all his problems? It came as an even bigger shock to them all when he suddenly collapsed and was rushed to hospital.

One Sunday night, Mrs Webb received a telephone call from the hospital. Would she come over straight away? Mr Webb had had a thrombosis, and the prognosis was grim. Cliff and his mother rushed to the hospital to find Rodger Webb in an oxygen tent, fighting for his life. The very next morning he died.

The death of his father was a terrible blow for

Cliff, who had always enjoyed a very close and loving relationship with him.

"I just can't believe it," he told his sisters. "I mean, you know your parents are going to die some day, but when it actually happens, when you realise that your father is gone and you'll never see him again, that's when it really hits you."

Cliff suffered a devastating bereavement. Rodger Webb had been strict with his children, but he had also been a caring and supportive father. His death also had professional repercussions for Cliff. He had been an invaluable guide and confidant during the whole of Cliff's professional career in show business. Cliff had relied on his dad to help him plan his work, and frequently talked through ideas and problems with him. Now he had to get by without his advice and encouragement.

In the period after his father's death, Cliff was overwhelmed by a terrible emptiness. For the first six months, he was working in Australia, so homesickness may have contributed to this feeling. Although he was able to carry on with his work, and he usually enjoyed himself when he was on stage, afterwards he wondered what the point of it all was.

The worst thing was that he couldn't understand why he was so unhappy. "If only I knew why these awful feelings take me over," he thought, "then I might be able to cope."

The idea occurred to him that if he could "get in touch" with his dead father, he might be able to ask him a few questions, just as he had done when he was alive. Cliff resolved to go to a spiritualist seance in the hope of making contact with his dad. One night he happened to mention this to Brian "Licorice" Locking, who was at that time bass player in the "Shadows". He was surprised by his friend's reaction.

"I really don't think you should do that," warned Brian.

"Why ever not?" asked Cliff.

"Don't you know it's extremely dangerous to mess around with spirits?"

Licorice produced a Bible from his pocket and proceeded to read out verses from the Old Testament prohibiting contact with spirits or mediums.

In the course of their conversation it emerged that Licorice was a devout Jehovah's Witness, a fact of which Cliff had not been aware, although he did have an inkling that his friend was religious. He was surprised to find that Brian took his faith so seriously and knew the Bible so well.

Finding guidance in the Bible was a new idea to Cliff. Up till then it had never occurred to him that such a dry and dusty old book might have something relevant to say about everyday life. "Maybe there's more to this than I thought," he concluded. "I must read some more."

He unearthed a copy of the Bible which he had at home and attempted to read it by himself. Unfortunately it turned out to be the King James Version (which is also known as the Authorised Version) and Cliff found the archaic language a struggle to read.

Turning to Brian for advice, he was given a copy of the Jehovah's Witnesses' translation of the Bible, the New World Bible, which had the advantage of being written in twentieth-century English. Cliff diligently read a chapter a day.

He also went with Brian to Jehovah's Witness meetings in Kingdom Halls throughout the country, along with Hank and Brian Bennett, who had some involvement with the sect. In addition, the four of them held Bible studies in their dressing room in Blackpool, while they were doing their summer season.

Excited about the new discoveries he was making, Cliff told his family all about the Jehovah's Witnesses, with the result that his mother and sisters also became involved. In fact, Jackie was eventually baptised into the sect and worked for them full-time for a spell.

Jehovah's Witnesses believe that God is one and that Jesus Christ was not divine, contrary to the

Christian doctrine of the Trinity. They believe that when God reigns on earth, the Witnesses will be rulers of the nations, but they maintain that only 144,000 believers will be saved. What particularly appealed to Cliff was the fact that their teaching was tremendously unified. You could go to any Kingdom Hall and hear exactly the same message being preached. To someone like Cliff, who liked everything to be straightforward, this was clearly an advantage.

Cliff's explorations were to take many months. One reason for his slow progress was partly due to the busy schedule that he and the Shadows had during that period. As well as the show in Blackpool, they were booked to do a long season at the Palladium in London, television work, records and overseas tours.

Although Cliff came to believe the teachings of the Jehovah's Witnesses, and defended them vigorously against criticism, he still held back from making a total commitment to the group. Even after two years of studying, discussing and attending meetings, he was reluctant to take the final step of being baptised into the faith, although his friends encouraged him to do so.

"Cliff, you believe our teachings, don't you?" asked Brian one day, as they were leaving a meeting.

"Of course," said Cliff.

"Then why not go ahead and get baptised?"

"It's not that easy," replied Cliff. "You know what would happen. It would be in all the newspapers, and how would my fans react?"

"So that's it? You think it might damage your career?"

"Well, it might do, and I'm not quite ready to take that risk," replied Cliff.

Nowadays Cliff would regard his fascination for the Jehovah's Witnesses as misguided and dangerous, but at least they helped him to start reading the Bible, to think about religious questions, and to discuss them. In short, they were the ones who set him off on his religious quest.

As it turned out, the next step in Cliff's pilgrimage was to alter his direction radically. In July 1965 Cliff was invited to take part in one of the car rallies which his former English teacher, Jay Norris, held every year to celebrate her birthday. Cliff's fourteen-year-old sister, Joan, was terribly excited at this as she knew her new class teacher, Mr Latham, would be going, and she desperately wanted Cliff to meet him.

Jay Norris also wanted Cliff to meet Bill Latham, but for a different reason. Cliff had told her all about his Jehovah's Witness beliefs, and she was uneasy about them, but being only a nominal Roman Catholic, she didn't feel equipped to explain her reservations. However she thought that Bill Latham, who was head of Religious Education at her school, could help Cliff find the answers he was looking for.

And so it was that on the day of the rally, Cliff found himself a passenger in Bill Latham's car. On that particular occasion they got on very well together, but to Jay's disappointment they didn't discuss religion at all. Nevertheless, a few months later, Cliff entertained Bill, Jay, and another teacher, Graham Disbrey, at his rather grand home in Nazeing.

That time, the conversation did get round to religion. Bill was an Anglican and Graham a Baptist, but both shared a common "orthodox" Christian outlook, and both were eager to convince Cliff that the Jehovah's Witnesses did not have all the answers. Of course, Cliff vigorously defended the Jehovah's Witness beliefs that he had learned during the previous two years.

To begin with, Cliff wasn't convinced by the arguments his new Christian friends put forward. Not everything Bill and Graham said sounded logical to him. One particular stumbling block was the Christian belief in the Trinity, as Cliff felt that all the explanations of this doctrine were far too vague.

However, there was something about Bill and Graham that impressed Cliff, so he gladly accepted a return invitation to visit Bill at his home in Finchley. This time, Bill had also invited David Winter, the editor of a Christian magazine, who later became Head of Religious Radio programmes at the BBC. An exceptional communicator, David was able to explain fundamental beliefs clearly and concisely.

"Christianity isn't just about knowing facts about Jesus," said David. "It's about knowing Jesus Himself, and having a personal relationship with Him."

"OK," said Cliff, "how do you do that then?"

"Admit that you are a sinner," he replied, "believe that Jesus died so that you can be forgiven, and trust in Him as your Saviour."

Christianity was beginning to make sense to Cliff, but again it was the people rather than the beliefs that inspired him. "They talk about Jesus as if they know Him," he reflected afterwards. "To them believing in Jesus is much more than going to church. It's a real relationship."

Bill continued to introduce Cliff to Christian teaching. He wisely invited him to attend a Sunday afternoon Crusaders class. As Cliff hadn't been to church for years, he might have found a visit to church intimidating; to attend a meeting in a hall with a lot of little boys was not nearly so threatening.

Crusaders was a kind of Christian club for boys

between the ages of eight and eighteen, and its programme included outings and camps and cruises on the Norfolk Broads as well as Sunday Bible classes. Bill Latham was leader of a local branch in Finchley.

Cliff found his first Sunday meeting with thirty or so fascinated boys slightly embarrassing. "What on earth am I doing here in the back row of an old classroom, reading the Bible with a bunch of small boys?" he asked himself. "If only my friends in the music business could see me now. They'd think I'd gone stark raving mad."

The boys, for their part, weren't sure how to cope with having a major pop star in their midst. Some were excited, others overawed, and there were the inevitable few who wanted to show off. But after a few meetings they soon regarded Cliff Richard as just another member of the class. Rugby tackles and horse play on one of the Crusader trips to the Norfolk Broads soon broke down any barriers that might have remained between Cliff and the lads.

The Crusaders club may have been a far cry from the rest of Cliff's pop star life, but he enjoyed being with ordinary people who related to him as a person, not just as a star. He was used to people wanting to get to know him because he was famous, not because they were interested in him as a person. It was a pleasant change for him to be able to relax with his Christian friends and simply be himself.

Cliff began to discover that Christian worship bore little resemblance to the turgid church services he remembered from his childhood. But even more amazing was the idea that someone could have a personal relationship with the living Christ.

For a year Cliff continued to read the Bible (this time, the New English Bible translation), to attend Crusaders, and to discuss Christianity, while still clinging tenuously to his Jehovah's Witness beliefs. One night at a Whitsun camp at Lewes, Cliff was having a vigorous argument with Bill, who by now was a good friend. Bill asked Cliff a question that really put him on the spot.

"Cliff, it's all very well to argue about doctrines, but tell me this," asked Bill, "how do you know you're saved?"

For Cliff it was the crunch question that completely undermined his loyalty to the Jehovah's Witnesses. As he struggled to answer it, he realised that Bill and the other Christians had something that the Jehovah's Witnesses didn't. Whereas the latter could only offer a collection of dogmas, Cliff's Christian friends could point to their personal relationship with Jesus. That was their assurance.

A few weeks later, Cliff became a Christian. At

the time he was staying at Bill's house in Finchley, to cut down on his travelling time to Pinewood Studios, where he was filming *Finders Keepers*. One evening he was reading the Book of Revelation, when he was struck by the words of Jesus, "Behold, I stand at the door and knock; whoever hears my voice and opens the door, I will come in."

That was the answer Cliff had been looking for. The Bible passage told him that Jesus had always been there, knocking, wanting to establish a relationship with Cliff, but Cliff had never given Jesus a chance. Now he knew what to do. His long search for the truth had reached an end. In bed that night, Cliff made a commitment. His prayer was nothing elaborate – just a simple, but sincere, invitation to Jesus to come in and take over his life.

Cliff's conversion may not have been particularly dramatic. He saw no visions, heard no heavenly voices. All he did was to utter a quiet prayer. But that simple act of faith was to turn his life upside down.

From that moment Cliff would live, not for himself, but for Jesus, whatever that might entail. His search for an answer had reached an end. But his new life with Jesus had only just begun.

5.

NEW LIFE?

Cliff might have expected his new-found Christian faith to bring him peace of mind and provide him with a smooth pathway through the complexities of life. In fact, it did just the opposite. Having found an answer to one of the biggest mysteries in the universe, Cliff was faced with yet another puzzle. What was he meant to do with his life?

It wasn't as if his career was floundering. Far from it. Professionally, he was just as busy as ever, and now his diary had some extra appointments in it — his various Christian activities. His happy involvement with Bill Latham's Crusader group continued, although Cliff was taken aback at being elected a leader.

"I'd consider it an honour, Bill, but I must admit I don't really feel I deserve it. You and the other guys put in far more hours than I do. I try to get to meetings as often as I can, but . . ."

"No need for apologies, Cliff. It isn't quantity that counts — it's quality. You should know that.

You give a lot of yourself to those boys. And they respond. They listen to you.''

As well as being involved in organised Christian activities, Cliff decided he would read part of his Bible every night. He felt that was top priority if he was to grow as a Christian, because he had such a lot to learn. However, he didn't find Bible reading too much of a problem, because he had already begun to study the scriptures some time ago, in the days when he was beginning to think about religion.

The real stumbling block was church. Cliff's previous experiences of church services were confined to singing in the choir as a boy in India, and going along with his mum to her church at Cheshunt when he was a teenager. Both of these had been fairly dismal experiences which had left him with the idea that church is gloomy and uninspiring. Cliff was afraid that all organised worship would be as dull and turgid as that and would not reflect the life and vitality he had discovered in Christianity.

There was an added complication to his relationship with the Church. In the days when he was looking for the element that was missing from his life, Cliff had become very involved with the Jehovah's Witnesses. Along with his fellow Shadow, Brian Locking, he attended many of the group's meetings, and spent hours listening to their teaching – far more attentively than he had ever listened to the sermons at his mum's old church. Although he was now a committed Christian, Cliff's mind was still steeped in Jehovah's Witness views, and it was going to take quite some time before these were replaced by more ''orthodox'' notions.

Bill Latham introduced Cliff into St Paul's, the Anglican church in Finchley where he himself was a lay reader, and did all he could to help him, but Cliff found his first few months as a churchgoer extremely trying. Every Sunday service, Cliff's Jehovah's Witness friends were at the back of his mind, warning him that churches were the work of the devil, so it was virtually impossible for him to relax and worship whole-heartedly with his fellow Christians. And every sermon he heard was a potential battlefield, because he disagreed with so many of the doctrines that were being taught. In the early days, he was particularly perplexed by Christian teaching on the Trinity, as it directly contradicted the ideas he had heard in the Jehovah's Witnesses' Halls.

Church took some getting used to, but so did the changes that were happening in Cliff's family. His sister Donna was now married, and there were another two family weddings in the offing. The first of these was his sister Jacqueline's. More surprising was his mother's marriage to the family's former chauffeur, Derek Bodkin, who at twenty-four was not much older than Cliff. The press tried to capitalise on the couple's age difference, and to make out that Cliff disapproved of the match. But to Cliff, his mother's happiness was far more important than any preconceived ideas about age, so he gladly gave the couple his blessing. When Dorothy and Derek told Cliff that they wanted to leave his rambling house and begin married life in a home of their own, Cliff very generously bought them a house as a wedding present.

With the rest of the family gone, it was no longer practical for Cliff to live alone in his massive Nazeing mansion, so he thought he might as well sell the property and get himself a small house or a flat. However, before he could find something suitable, a better solution suggested itself. He heard that Bill Latham and his mother were planning to move. Why didn't the three of them share a house? After all, Cliff had already stayed with them for quite some time when he was filming, and they had all got on very well together. A suitable Georgian style house was found just down the road from Finchley in Totteridge, and it made a cosy home for Cliff and his second family.

As time went by, Cliff's misgivings about churchgoing receded, and he eventually felt able to commit himself, not just to Jesus, but to His people, the Church, in the shape of the Church of England. He was confirmed in his own church on 6th December 1966 by the Bishop of Willesden. It was an important step for Cliff, a chance for him to accept for himself the promises made by his parents at his baptism, to be welcomed into the family of the Church, and to declare his faith publicly.

Not that Cliff's faith was terribly public at this stage! Bill Latham had made sterling efforts to keep the story of Cliff's conversion out of the press, and by and large he had succeeded. Occasionally there was an article about Cliff's Christian faith, like the interview in the London *Evening Standard* in December 1965, in which the singer talked about his work with the Crusader group, but somehow or other his conversion had escaped being sensationalised by the mass media.

Christian groups, however, were well aware of Cliff's new-found faith, and eagerly requested him to come and speak about his experiences and his beliefs. Often he would visit an individual congregation or a youth group and tell them the story of his conversion, but he took part in some extremely large gatherings as well. In April 1966, he was interviewed at the Central Hall, Westminster in front of 2,700 Christians, and on another occasion he sang and played his guitar at a Crusader rally in the same building. In each case, Cliff was able to rise to the occasion as he was used to big audiences and his youth work had equipped him to communicate with crowds of youngsters.

Then came an invitation to another big Christian rally, but this particular one was to have tremendous repercussions on his life. Billy Graham, the famous American evangelist, had been intrigued to hear about this British rock star who had recently become a Christian, and he invited Cliff to give a public testimony of his faith at a big revival meeting at Earls Court in London.

Cliff knew that if he accepted this invitation, it wouldn't simply be a matter of another public appearance. Billy Graham's Greater London Crusade had aroused considerable interest among Christian circles, and Cliff had already gone with some members of his church youth group to hear the great man speak. He had a deep respect for the preacher, who took the Bible's authority very seriously, and he was thrilled to see so many people come forward during the meeting and offer their lives to Jesus. Yes, Cliff believed Billy Graham's evangelistic crusade was definitely a good way to get people to think about Jesus.

But he was also well aware of the fact that Dr Graham was a religious leader of international repute, and that his crusades were the focus of considerable media attention. Add to that the novelty of a famous pop star making a public declaration of his recent religious conversion, and it was obvious that the press would have a field day. Cliff knew that he wouldn't just be talking to the 25,000 who would attend the rally. If he went ahead and accepted the invitation to speak, he would be telling the whole world that he was a Christian. And if he did, there would be plenty of people only too glad to point a finger at him the minute he stepped out of line.

"What do you think then, Cliff?" asked Bill, his eyes full of concern. "If do you go and speak at this rally, there's no turning back, you know that. Are you sure that's what you really want?"

"I am," said Cliff quietly. "I know it's a big step, and I'm terrified. I could take a lot of stick for it – it could even mean the end of my career. But what sort of a Christian would I be if I refused?"

By the day of the rally, 16th June 1966, word had got around that Cliff would be giving his testimony, and press and fans crowded into the stadium along with those who genuinely wanted to hear the speakers' message. Two thousand five hundred souls were gathered there, some already Christians, some just interested to find out more, others curious to hear how Cliff had "found religion".

Cliff's mind was in turmoil as he looked out on to the sea of expectant faces. This time there was no role to hide behind; it was the real Cliff that the public would see, not some celluloid fantasy. By the time he heard his name being announced, he was beginning to wish he had stayed at home. Cliff, the star of stage and screen, who would happily sing, dance, or act in front of any audience, discovered that his composure had suddenly vanished.

As he stumbled towards the lectern, he was shocked to find that his legs would hardly carry him. The young man, who was usually so agile on stage, was now so tense that his whole body had gone rigid. He clutched the lectern for dear life, took a deep breath, and opened his mouth. He didn't even recognise the sound of his own voice, the voice that pop fans all over the country knew so well. But somehow the words seemed to come.

"I have never had the opportunity to speak to an audience as big as this before, but it is a great privilege to be able to tell so many people that I am a Christian."

He had started. He felt a huge wave of peace flood through his body. His heart was still pounding, and his arms were still rigid, but it was all right. He was telling the world about the most deeply personal experience of his life, making himself frighteningly vulnerable, but it was all right – everything would be all right. God was giving him the strength to go through with it.

"I can only say to people who are not Christians that until you have taken the step of asking Christ into your life, your life is not really worthwhile. It works – it works for me!"

While the crowd reflected on what he had told them, Cliff began to sing, very quietly, It is no secret what God can do". And the words were true. It was no longer a secret that God had come into Cliff Richard's life and changed it totally.

It was an enormous relief for Cliff to have brought his Christian faith out into the open at last – he knew it was the right thing to do – but the media's response to the meeting confirmed that Bill had been right to worry about the effects of such a revelation. Suddenly Cliff's conversion was the favourite talking point of members of the press, who eagerly pieced together any snippets of information they could grab hold of.

At the same time, Cliff had his own preoccupations. Since his conversion, he had been thinking really hard about whether he should continue with his career in the music business. Many of his new friends, including Bill Latham and Graham Disbrey, were teachers, and Cliff couldn't help thinking that their jobs were more worthwhile than his own. There he was on stage or in the television studio, doing a job that was a lot of fun, and being paid vast sums of money for the privilege. It didn't seem right! Cliff began to wonder whether he would be able to contribute more to society if he changed to a more "normal" job.

Perhaps if he had felt more certain about where he was going in his show business career, Cliff would not have felt compelled to go off and try his hand at something else. But that was one of his problems – professionally, he didn't have any new challenges to strive for. Although he was still a very young man, he had already fulfilled more ambitions than most people do in a lifetime. He was a success in the record industry, in television, and in films. What was there left for him to achieve?

But the urge to move on to a different line of work wasn't due only to Cliff's aimlessness. As far as his future plans were concerned, Cliff believed he didn't just have to follow his own needs and desires. He was a Christian, and so he had to ask himself, "What is it that God wants me to do?" His career was a wonderful gift from God – how many other people had such a glamorous and lucrative job? – but did it occupy too big a place in Cliff's heart? If God really wanted him to give up everything – the fame, the fortune, the prestige – would he love Him enough to do that? Cliff has never been one to pay lip service to his religion, and he wanted to be sure that he was acting from the purest of motives, not just from self-interest.

Cliff's Crusade appearance may have been the event that brought his conversion into the public eye, but even before that the young man had been thinking about leaving show business. In the *Evening Standard* in December 1965, he told Maureen Cleave that he was considering giving up his successful career. "At the moment I feel dissatisfied. I don't get the same kick out of my life as I used to. I always said that if I didn't feel completely happy I would retire. I feel I could do more with my life."

As long ago as that he had been thinking of going into teaching, and he had even tried to find out whether it would be a feasible option. "I would have to go to college for two years because I only got English Language in G.C.E. but then I would be equipped to teach English and Religious Education."

But there was still the question of whether he would, in fact, be awarded a place at teacher training college. The stumbling block was that he had very few academic qualifications, because he had been terrified of examinations. Cliff had always done reasonably well in his class work, but ever since his fateful "eleven-plus" exam, he had never been able to do himself justice under exam conditions.

However his chosen training college was more flexible in its entry requirements than Cliff had anticipated. The principal reassured him that it wasn't just pieces of paper that mattered. The college always had a place for people who really wanted to teach, and Cliff's willingness to sacrifice fame and fortune to go into the profession, and his previous commitment to young people through the Crusaders were proof enough of that.

Although the college had confidence in him, Cliff still had some niggling doubts that he wouldn't be able to cope with the academic content of the course, so he decided to take an "O" level in Religious Education to see how he would get on with the business of studying. With Bill's help he managed to pass the exam, but in the process he discovered that he wasn't very keen on the self-discipline that all students need. Being stuck at a desk and having to plough through books and write essays just didn't come naturally to him. All those bits of paper reminded him too much of his dreadful clerical job at Atlas Lamps.

Cliff was beginning to realise it wouldn't be easy to carve out a new career as a teacher. A lesser person might just have given up on the idea for the sake of an easy life, but Cliff was still convinced that he had to push ahead with his plans to change careers. He had to do his best for God, whatever the personal cost.

All the time that Cliff was wrestling with the problem of his future career, he was under the pressure of constant media scrutiny. Many reporters saw Cliff's change of course as a terrific story and they were determined to get as much mileage out of it as they could. It made it all the harder for Cliff to think clearly about his life, when every time he opened a newspaper he found yet more speculation about his future.

Then there was a different kind of pressure from his army of fans, who were beginning to panic about losing their pop idol to school-teaching. They begged him to reconsider, to stay put in show business, to remain the same old Cliff that they had loved for so long. Some of them even drew up petitions to protest against their hero's retirement. How could he resist their pleas?

But Cliff's mind was made up. He went ahead with the necessary steps to disband his fan club, in spite of all the members' protests. All he had to do now was make his decision final. He called a press conference to end the speculation once and for all. At last, the journalists had their scoop. Cliff Richard would definitely be quitting show business – and that was official!

At the end of the meeting, Cliff felt an anxious gnawing in the pit of his stomach. He had been so sure that this step was what God wanted, but could he have possibly been mistaken? He turned to Peter Gormley, his manager, for reassurance.

"Am I doing the right thing, Peter? Am I right to give all this up?"

"If that's what you want, Cliff, then that's what you should do. What sort of a career do you think you'll have if your heart isn't in it one hundred percent?"

It was a good point. It's extremely difficult to succeed in the tough world of show business, even if the performer is totally dedicated to his art. Cliff knew deep down that if he was no longer committed to his singing career, he would be wasting his time to try to carry on with it.

Peter Gormley stressed that the decision must be Cliff's, but some of Cliff's other friends were still adamant that it would be a mistake for him to give up his career and go into teaching. Even after he had officially announced his retirement and it seemed that there was no turning back, they still tried to make him change his mind. Cliff received a great deal of advice from his various Christian friends, including David Winter and John Stott. But it was Jim Collier, the man who was to direct him in the Billy Graham film, *Two a Penny*, who finally helped Cliff to see that God didn't require him to give up his career.

"Cliff," he argued, "why on earth does

everyone think they have to give up their jobs when they become converted? Don't you understand that God wants us to be Christians right where we are?''

Suddenly Cliff did understand. He didn't need to quit show business in order to be a Christian. God had work for him to do right where he was, in his career as an entertainer. Cliff hurriedly called an eleventh hour halt to his retirement plans and, as if to prove the point, there suddenly arose a host of marvellous new opportunities for him to communicate his faith.

Television was one means of communication to which Cliff, as a public figure, had access, and this was a great privilege. Cliff was invited to defend his faith on several television programmes, including one made by ABC Television, in which he was pitted against another pop singer, Paul Jones, formerly lead singer in a group called Manfred Man. The two protagonists were meant to argue on opposite sides about the case for Christianity, but they were not evenly matched. Jones had been to university and was highly articulate, whereas Cliff was bright and enthusiastic but he had never been trained in the art of debate. Although Jones had the advantage intellectually, viewers were impressed by the sincerity of Cliff's faith, which shone through the whole of the debate. Ironically, Paul Jones was himself to become a committed Christian many years later.

Cliff was also inundated with requests for magazine interviews. Through the medium of magazines, he was able to make his Christian views known to many ordinary people who might not otherwise have heard about religion. He also continued to speak at lots of youth gatherings and adult meetings.

Before long, Cliff was witnessing to so many people in such a wide range of situations that he wondered how he could ever have been so naive as to contemplate leaving show business. Clearly, he didn't need to give up his existing career to spread God's word. All he had to do was stay where he was, and the opportunities would come to him.

6.

NEARLY FAMOUS

"You know, Bill," said Cliff one day, as he was looking through his week's appointments, "ever since all that retirement business, I've been getting terrific opportunities to speak about my faith."

"And to think you nearly passed them all up to become a school-teacher! I bet you're glad you stayed where you are!"

"You can say that again! But isn't it strange. I was right at the point when I was ready to give it all up, and it was only then that God said, 'Hold on, we'll use your career'."

Cliff was thrilled when he was asked to appear in one of Billy Graham's films, *Two a Penny*. The film company, Worldwide Films, were looking for a Christian English actor with film experience to play the lead, and Cliff jumped at the chance to prove his acting ability in a straight role. Unfortunately, as the film was never given a general release, it was only shown in church halls and meeting rooms throughout the country.

Nevertheless, Cliff regarded it as "far and away the best film" he had ever done.

As Cliff's Christian engagements grew, he found it increasingly difficult to keep track of his busy schedule. He had his management team of Peter Gormley, David Bryce, and a few others to organise his professional schedules, but now there was the question of who would get him to his church meetings on time, liaise with clergy about visits, and reply to requests for personal appearances. Organisation was never one of Cliff's strong points, and, besides, he didn't really have the time to do lots of administration.

Fortunately his friend Bill Latham was willing to step in and take responsibility for arranging Cliff's Christian activities. To begin with, these extra duties resulted in a very heavy work load for Bill, who was still working full-time as a teacher. In the evenings, when he got home from school after a hard day's work, he would often spend another two or three hours replying to Cliff's post and sorting out his schedules. After a while, Bill gave up teaching to take up a post with the relief agency, TEAR Fund, but he still continued to organise Cliff's Christian activities.

To begin with, Cliff's Christian appearances were fairly simple and low-key. He would attend church services and Crusader classes in various parts of the country, sing a few gospel songs, and tell people about his faith. But after a while, the invitations began to snowball, and he started to speak at universities and cathedrals as well. As his confidence grew, he enlisted Bill's help to put on a question-and-answer presentation, and he even allowed questions from the floor. Cliff found this far more effective than reciting a set piece, as it enabled him to be more spontaneous. He felt that practising a speech over and over again took all the life from it.

Cliff's religious activities were thriving, but his show business career was equally buoyant. In the year after Cliff decided not to leave show business, he was chosen to represent Britain in the Eurovision Song Contest, an annual competition in which several countries enter a song of their choice, and the winner, the "Song for Europe", is chosen. Hundreds of millions of people watch it on television, as it is transmitted to all the participating countries. The 1968 competition was to be held in the Royal Albert Hall in London – a great confidence booster for Britain – and the song which Cliff was to sing, a bouncy number called "Congratulations", was one of the favourites.

When the British contestant came on stage and the orchestra played the opening notes, the atmosphere was electric. Cliff belted out the song enthusiastically, and the audience in the Albert Hall were soon tapping their feet to the catchy rhythm. They liked it, there was no doubt about that. The song had already been tipped for the prize, and hopes were high. By the time all the contestants had performed their entries, it was clear that "Congratulations" was a hot contender for first place.

The juries from the participating countries began to award points to the songs they had liked best. It was a nail-biting time for Cliff, and he could hardly bear to listen, but he knew that there were a lot of people willing him to win — his crowd of supporters in the Albert Hall and the millions of Britons watching at home. The voting was going well, very well — victory was within grasp. He didn't dare think about it. But when the last jury announced its verdict, there was a gasp of surprise from the audience. The Spanish song, "La, La, La", had edged into the lead, to win by one point, one single point.

It was a terrible disappointment for Cliff, as he and so many other people had been sure that "Congratulations" would win. Even the compere, Katie Boyle, demanded a recount, because she couldn't believe the final result. However, she was full of admiration for the way in which Cliff coped with such a terrible blow. "I've seen 'good losers' before, but never one who sailed through the experience with not a flicker of disappointment on his face," she remembered.

However, there were compensations for the gallant loser. Even though Congratulations had lost the contest, the record still managed to top the charts in Britain and abroad – in Germany it managed to occupy the number one slot for an astounding seven weeks. Sales of the record rocketed over the million mark, resulting in a fifth Gold Disc for Cliff.

Throughout the next decade, Cliff was to become a familiar figure on British television. He appeared so regularly during that period that, for many people, he became part of their everyday lives, a fixed point in their weekly routine. During the winter months of the seventies, many people's long, dark Saturday evenings were brightened up by watching Cliff's weekly TV show. In 1971 and 1972, he had a thirteen-week television series of his own, and he appeared in several other television and radio programmes as well, including a complicated TV play called *The Case*.

In the 1972 series of *It's Cliff Richard*, the New Seekers were Cliff's musical guests for several weeks. They were to take part in that year's Eurovision Song Contest, and it was on Cliff's show that they performed the final six songs from which viewers would select one to be the British entry.

The following year, Cliff himself was chosen to represent Britain in the contest for a second time, and so he appeared as a guest on Cilla Black's BBC1 series for six consecutive weeks, singing the short-listed entries. Experts reckoned that the viewers' choice, ''Power to All Our Friends'', was a strong entry and prophesied that it stood a good chance of becoming the next Song for Europe. Would Cliff's second stab at the Eurovision contest be more successful than his first?

Cliff found it every bit as nerve-racking to represent Britain second time around – possibly even more so. True, he had a better idea of what he was letting himself in for, but he also knew that, no matter how good your song was, there was no guarantee that it would win. But he wanted to win, to make up for his failure last time. He was lucky to get a second chance – he might not get another one.

But, again, it was not to be. This time, Cliff came third, behind the Spanish entry and the winning Luxembourg ballad, ''Un Banc, Un Arbre, Une Rue''. It was another bitter blow for Cliff, and it must have been extremely difficult for him to conceal his disappointment from the four hundred million people who were watching the competition on television. But the people around him were surprised to see that Cliff was apparently more concerned for the songwriters than he was for himself. The writers of "Power to All Our Friends", Guy Fletcher and Doug Flett, recall that "Cliff was terribly apologetic, as though it had something to do with him."

The British singer and songwriters found some consolation in the song's commercial success. It may have only reached third place in the Eurovision Song Contest, but the single of "Power to All Our Friends" reached the Top Five in fourteen countries, won coveted Gold Disks, and was Cliff's biggest hit since "Congratulations".

In 1974 Cliff was back on BBC television with another series of *It's Cliff Richard*, this time featuring an all-girl pop group called the Nolan Sisters. It was a bad year for Cliff health-wise, as he was plagued with laryngitis, bronchitis, and back trouble, but that didn't stop his busy schedule of media appearances and tours.

Cliff's many television appearances were beginning to give Cliff a new identity. By the mid-1970s the public was inclined to think of him as a general entertainer instead of a rock'n'roll singer. His 1975 series, *It's Cliff – And Friends*, featured a variety of guests, including many comedians, and was very definitely a family entertainment show rather than a pop music programme. Some people were beginning to wonder whether Cliff was drifting away from his rock'n'roll roots?

Around that time, Cliff himself was unsure about the direction he wanted his career to go in. He had been interested in drama for many years, and now he wondered whether he should devote more of his attention to acting instead of singing. But he was by no means certain he wanted to give up his first love, pop music, which still fascinated him. It was a difficult decision, but in the end the music won, and Cliff renewed his commitment to his rock'n'roll roots.

If anyone had harboured any doubts about Cliff's identity as a pop singer, several events in 1976 confirmed that Cliff was still a figure to be reckoned with in the music business. During that year he had so many musical successes that one music paper dubbed it ''the year of the Cliff Richard renaissance''.

Suddenly Cliff was popular again as a pop singer, and it was mainly due to his outstanding new album, ''I'm Nearly Famous'', recorded in the famous Abbey Road studio where the Beatles had made their records. Three of the songs from ''I'm Nearly Famous'' became hit singles in dozens of countries, and the album put Cliff back into the album charts for the first time in years. His ambitious vocal treatment of ''Miss You Nights'' and ''I Can't Ask for Anything More, Babe'' proved that Cliff had finally developed the confidence to sing in his own style, and showed the world that he was more than just another Elvis soundalike.

Cliff was particularly proud of the third hit taken from the album, a song called "Devil Woman", which was his first single to reach the United States Top 10. Cliff's superstar friend, Elton John worked extremely hard at promoting both "Devil Woman" and "Miss You Nights" in the American market place, and his efforts paid off.

Some people criticised Cliff for recording "Devil Woman", on the grounds that its title had overtones of black magic. However, Cliff has always defended the song as a valid and exciting piece of music. He argues that the lyrics are completely moral; in fact, they warn people against the dangers of devil worship rather than encouraging them to try it out.

Cliff has a striking example of how he believes the song was used by God to bring about good. A teenage girl had been suffering from a severe depression, and in her desperation, she was on the verge of turning to occult practices for comfort. Some of her Christian friends were very concerned about her welfare, and warned her of the dangers of the occult, but she wouldn't listen to them. But they knew she was a fan of Cliff Richard, so they persuaded her to listen to his record of "Devil Woman". The words of the song got through to her more effectively than the warnings of her friends. The distressed young woman steered clear of the occult, found a way to deal with her problems, and eventually became a Christian herself.

Another of Cliff's musical high spots that year was his Russian tour, in which he played eight concerts in Moscow and twelve in Leningrad at the request of the country's official State Entertainments Department, Gosconcerts. It was an historic event, as Cliff had the privilege of being the first Western rock star ever to play in the USSR. Naturally he was excited about this new venture, but as the three-week tour approached, he felt more and more apprehensive about it. The Russian authorities had a reputation for being tough censors and keeping tight control over any political or religious material. Cliff was worried that the powers that be might take exception to some of his gospel songs and force him to cut the words, which he would have not have wanted to do.

But when he got to Russia, he found that the authorities didn't bat an eyelid at any of his Christian songs. The only material they quibbled with was a verse from a song called "Love Train", a "Philadelphia" number, which contained a politically sensitive reference to the people of Russia, China and Israel joining hands together.

Pessimists had also warned Cliff that his Moscow audience would be packed with sedate and elderly officials who would applaud out of politeness rather than excitement, so it was not surprising that Cliff's heart was in his boots when he stepped on stage in Leningrad for the first of his concerts.

He needn't have worried. The Russian audiences were every bit as enthusiastic as the fans back home in England. Many of the Leningrad fans even tried to climb on stage and hug Cliff and his companions, so on subsequent nights the organisers had to open up the orchestra pit to prevent people from swarming the stage! The Moscow audiences were equally appreciative, eager to enjoy the country's "first real taste of rock'n'roll". Even the Russian news agency Tass gave glowing reports of the British rock shows.

But it was Cliff's contact with Russian Christians that made the Soviet tour an unforgettable experience. Cliff had heard that Christians in Russia were not allowed to practise their religion as freely as their Western counterparts. He was eager to worship with them and see for himself what it was like to be a Christian in a communist country. One Sunday morning he attended a service at Moscow Baptist Church, where he experienced a unity with his fellow believers that transcended any barriers of politics or language.

As Cliff entered the packed church, he was surprised to find that there were very few hymn books in the building – only about one between twenty people.

"Is this really all they have?" Cliff asked incredulously, squeezing his way into the visitors' pew.

"Yes," replied his Russian escort. "Under Russian law all printed material is strictly monitored and controlled."

"How on earth do they manage to sing the hymns then?"

"It's no problem. Wait and see!"

Cliff discovered that in between every verse of a hymn, the minister would stop the congregation and read them the words of the next verse. It seemed to work, as everyone was joining in enthusiastically with the singing, except for Cliff, who couldn't understand a single word. But, in spite of the language barrier, he could tell that the Russian Christians were worshipping with all their hearts and he was soon caught up in the joyful atmosphere.

The worship was much more intense than it was in churches back home, which made it all the more frustrating that Cliff couldn't join in fully. If only he could speak Russian! He didn't know what to do. The choir master graciously invited Cliff to sing a solo, but the British guest reluctantly declined. Cliff has always felt that his voice won't work properly first thing in the morning, and he hates to give anyone less than his best.

Fortunately the choir master persisted with his request, and the Russian congregation fell silent as Cliff began to sing the lovely old hymn, ''When I survey the wondrous cross'', his voice brimming with emotion. At last, words didn't matter. He and his fellow Christians understood each other perfectly.

7.

NO LONGER AN ISLAND

Cliff had heard a lot about the suffering of the refugees in Bangladesh, but nothing had prepared him for the terrible reality of the Bihari refugee camp. Everywhere he looked there were starving children, disease-ridden bodies, faces racked with grief and desperation. He had witnessed more pain in his first few minutes at the camp than he had done in the whole of his lifetime.

He was beginning to wonder whether he had been right to come here. It had been Bill's idea. Cliff's friend, Bill Latham, was now Education Secretary of a charity called TEAR Fund, which provides relief for people like these refugees. Bill and the Director of the charity, George Hoffman, were spending some time going round TEAR Fund projects in Bangladesh. As Cliff was travelling back from a visit to Australia at about that time, Bill had suggested that Cliff might like to break his journey and spend a week with them in the mission field.

"It will be good experience for you, Cliff," said

Bill. "And maybe you can do a soundstrip for TEAR Fund while you're out there."

"Anything to help. Bangladesh, eh? I expect it'll be a bit like going home," said Cliff, enthusiastically. "Back to my roots! Well, nearly!"

"I wouldn't be too sure about that," frowned Bill, "it isn't a holiday camp we're going to."

Cliff thought he had a pretty good idea of what Bangladesh would be like. After all, he had spent the first seven years of his childhood in India – surely Bangladesh wasn't that different? The people, the countryside, the vegetation – he could visualise them all.

But life in this Bihari camp was nothing like the India of Cliff's childhood. Here there were none of the pleasures that he remembered so fondly. Balmy holidays spent fishing and kite-flying. The family servants bringing his favourite curry to the school-yard for his lunch. Being at home in the Webbs' comfortable apartment and popping downstairs to the chocolate factory for some free samples. These refugees knew nothing of the security and comfort that Cliff had enjoyed. It was the same continent, but a different world.

He wasn't sure he could stay much longer in this awful camp. He'd only been in the place an hour or two, but already he was longing to get away from it. He was nearly sick with the stench of stale urine and stinking bodies, and apparently this wasn't even the worst of the camps! At some of them, so the nurse had told him, they would need to wear Wellington boots, there was so much sewage to trudge through.

As for the refugees! He knew he ought to be friendly and loving but, to tell the truth, he couldn't even bear to be near them. Every last one of them was a festering mass of sores and scabs, even the tiniest baby. It made Cliff's stomach turn just to look at them – there was no way he could possibly bring himself to touch anybody. He was sure he was going to catch some ghastly disease before he got out of this place. Every time he found a well or tap he scrubbed his hands, trying to wash away the dirt and disease from his body, and perhaps from his mind as well.

Still, at least he had something useful to do for the next few minutes. The photographer had arrived to take some pictures for the sound strip. A few evocative shots of Cliff Richard with a refugee child might help to raise a bit of money for the poor souls. Better get it over with.

Cliff cautiously bent down beside one of the children and got ready to pose. But suddenly the hot air was filled with a piercing scream – someone had accidentally trodden on the child's hands. The little mite's face crumpled with pain, and Cliff instinctively put his arms around him, all his fears of infection forgotten. All that mattered at this moment was the tiny, tearful human being in front of him.

The child immediately stopped crying, and Cliff felt a surge of love and empathy towards him and all the other people in the camp. Cliff had brought comfort to a helpless child but, strangely enough, the child had done something valuable for him as well – he had broken through Cliff's emotional barriers by showing him that behind the sores and the scabs and the dirt were human beings with their own hopes and fears and feelings, who were in just as much need of love and care as the clean, healthy children of the West.

To witness the poverty and suffering of the refugees was doubly shocking for Cliff, because he had just left Australia, where he had been performing at the Sydney Opera House shortly after its official opening. Having just experienced the pristine luxury of the Opera House with its plush decor and abundance of champagne, he found the Bangladeshi refugee camps an obscene contrast. So too was the five-star Intercontinental Hotel where Cliff was staying, a million miles away, with its air-conditioned rooms and uniformed doorman, from the squalor and degradation of the destitute.

Looking around at babies with faces like old men, and women weeping for their dead children, Cliff felt as if his eyes were being opened for the first time. He had been so sure he understood what was going on in these refugee camps — after all, he'd spent hours listening to Bill and reading TEAR Fund literature — but somehow he had failed to grasp how grim the camps really were, and how desperately the people needed help.

As part of his Christian stewardship, Cliff had been giving financial support to camps such as these through TEAR Fund. The Evangelical Alliance Relief Fund, to give it its full name, had been founded with the twin, but related, aims of carrying out relief and development work and providing evangelical Christian witness. For a bible-based Christian like Cliff, it was the ideal charity to support. The young man admired the way in which it aimed to nourish people's souls as well as their bodies.

Cliff believed that he had a responsibility as a Christian to use his high earnings wisely, but he was keen to do this in an informed way, rather than just donate money to a charity that he knew virtually nothing about. When he heard about the work of TEAR Fund, he thought that here, at last, was an opportunity to get really involved with a worthwhile charity. He didn't have any first-hand experience of its work, but if it helped people spiritually as well as physically, then surely it was following Jesus' example.

Cliff knew in his mind that TEAR Fund was a

good cause, but at that time he didn't really have many deep feelings in his heart for the people he was helping. Not until he travelled across the world to Bangladesh and actually met some of the needy people and the staff who were trying to help them. Not until the distress of one small child got through to him.

TEAR Fund personnel work along with missionaries to relieve suffering and give Third World development projects whatever assistance is necessary. Sometimes they provide training in agriculture or set up schemes to provide a clean water supply for a village; or they may deal with a particular disaster, such as a flood, or an earthquake, or a famine. They also provide medical expertise, both preventative medicine and the kind of treatment that was desperately needed by the diseased and mal-nourished people at the Bihari refugee camps.

It was a humbling experience for Cliff to see the nurses and doctors in action in the field, and to realise how dedicated they must be to come and work for years in such atrocious conditions. Here in Bangladesh the staff were having to cope day in, day out, with the heat and the stench and the anguish, and they were giving people precisely the sort of help they needed. Without doubt, their contribution to the poor was Christian and sacrificial.

Cliff felt ashamed at how little he had given in comparison – how little he could do to help, even here at the camp. Back home in Britain Cliff was a major star, someone special who brought pleasure to thousands of people, but none of that seemed to matter here. What good was a famous singer to a man dying of malnutrition or a woman who had just lost her baby? It was food and medical attention that they needed, not entertainment.

Suddenly Cliff's own work, even his own efforts to support TEAR Fund, seemed terribly shallow. So what if he put on a few concerts and raised a bit of money for charity? Even though he might raise thousands of pounds through one of his concerts, it was nothing to be proud of. He always enjoyed himself when he was on stage – the sort of charity work he did was no real hardship. But things were different for these relief workers in Bangladesh. They were in the front line. The personal cost of their work was so much greater, and their contribution to the refugees' welfare was, in his eyes, far more significant.

He stood beside one of the nurses as she injected a sickly child. Cliff felt totally inadequate as he watched her.

"I feel such a fraud," he said. "It's so easy for me to raise money back home. But the real work is going on out here. Maybe I'd be doing more good if I packed everything in and came to work in one of these camps?''

The nurse raised a wary eyebrow and looked Cliff straight in the eye. ''Are you any good at giving injections?'' she asked.

''No,'' said Cliff.

''Then you wouldn't be much use out here, would you? But we do need people like you to stay in Britain and raise money. After all, we can't do anything here unless someone finds the money to pay for it.''

''I'd never thought of it like that,'' sighed Cliff. ''Maybe I should stick to what I know best after all.''

His thoughts returned to 1968 and the night he took part in his first concert for TEAR Fund, the Help, Hope and Hallelujah evening devised by David Winter. What an evening that had been! It was odd to be appearing without the Shadows and his favourite hit songs, but what a wonderful experience it was to be on stage with the Settlers folk group, singing gospel songs and choruses to such a large audience. And what a thrill it had been when they found out how much money they had raised — two thousand pounds, enough to send a badly-needed ambulance to South America!

Cliff was glad he had been able to raise some money for TEAR Fund, but at that time he never dreamed that he would one day visit one of the Fund's relief camps and see the valuable work which the agency was doing, and would continue to do, as long as there was enough money.

Now that he had been to Bangladesh, Cliff believed that the Third World was desperate for aid – and it was up to everyone to give what they could. It was no use giving up on the problems of poverty and disease and war, just because they seemed intractable. Surely it was better to do something, to save even a few lives, rather than sit back and not even try to help? The people of the West had so much, and there were so many people in the world who had nothing at all.

"Well, Cliff," said Bill at the end of the day, as he took the young man back to his hotel for a refreshing shower and a good night's sleep in clean, starched sheets, "are you finding your visit useful?"

"You bet your life I am," replied Cliff. "I don't think I'll ever be the same again. I only wish everybody could come out here and see the things that I've seen today – then they might put their hands in their pockets and help."

They nodded politely to the doorman of the Intercontinental as he opened a gleaming glass door for them.

Cliff paused in the gracious hotel foyer. The hotel was even more elegant than he remembered, and the air-conditioning was bliss after a sweaty day in the Bangladeshi sun. There was nothing wrong with staying in a nice hotel, was there? Yet he couldn't help thinking back to all the poor people he had seen who had no food, no bed, no roof over their head. To the disease and dirt and desperation of the camps. To the starving children and grieving mothers.

"I'll never forget this day, Bill. Not for as long as I live. And I'll never forget those people either."

8.

GET THE MESSAGE

"I hear last week's college meeting went very well, Cliff," said David Winter over coffee one evening.

"Terrific," said Cliff. "There was so much they wanted to know about Christianity. We could have talked all night."

David stared thoughtfully at his coffee cup.

"You've been spending quite a lot of time on question and answer sessions recently. You must find there are a lot of questions that people ask over and over again?"

"Sure," said Cliff, "loads."

Cliff had been taking part in question and answer session for schools and churches ever since his conversion. Later, after his visit to the TEAR Fund camps, he started to do gospel concerts in larger venues to raise money for various charities, and questions and answers were included in these as well. Cliff would sing some gospel songs, often accompanying himself on his guitar, and in between he would chat about Christianity with Bill Latham.

"Listen, Cliff," said David. "I've been thinking. Why don't you collect some of the typical questions you're asked along with your replies, and turn them into a book?"

Cliff looked sceptical. "You must be joking! Me write a book?"

"Well, you wouldn't exactly have to write it. You could chat away on a tape recorder about some of the typical questions people ask, then I would write it all down and tidy it up a bit. What do you think?"

"Well, I'm no expert, but if you think people would find it useful, I'll give it a try."

On the way home that night, Cliff couldn't stop thinking about David's idea. It was a good one. Cliff knew there were lots of things that people don't know about religion. All they needed was someone to answer their questions clearly and simply. But just imagine it! All the same he couldn't help smiling. Harry Webb writing a book! After all those dreadful exam results! Who'd have imagined it?

Bill Latham was delighted when Cliff told him about David's idea.

"About time too. You're a very good communicator in your own way. And think of all the people you could reach – people who wouldn't normally set foot inside a church.''

''We'd have to be careful about the title though,'' said Cliff. ''I'm no theologian and I wouldn't want people to think I was setting myself up as one. It would just be the way I see things.''

''That's your title then,'' said Bill. '' 'The Way I See It'!''

And so began another aspect of Cliff's remarkable career – his books which explain Christianity in everyday language. *The Way I See It* sold extremely well, not just in Britain but in dozens of countries throughout the world. It was followed by two other volumes in the same vein, *Questions*, and *The Way I See It Now*, but these were only the first in a long line of religious books, records, videos and cassettes about Christianity and the Bible.

For years Cliff had been getting his message across in person in meetings and gospel concerts, but he was now reaching millions of other people as well through his publications, which could be found in libraries and bookshops everywhere.

It was a winning combination – Cliff's down to earth approach and popular appeal together with David Winter's considerable media experience. But the books were never conceived as money spinners. They were simply a way to bring the Christian message to a wider range of people, an extension of the work Cliff already did face to face in meetings, interviews and gospel concerts.

Cliff liked to think of his Christian work as "pre-evangelism". He believed it wouldn't be appropriate for him, as a pop star, to bring people to the point of commitment in the public setting of a meeting or a gospel concert. The excitement, the glamour, the high emotional level of the event might distort people's true feelings and lead them to make a commitment for the wrong reasons, and that certainly wasn't Cliff's aim. Instead he hoped his books, gospel concerts and Christian meetings would get people talking and thinking about Christianity. They could make their minds up later when they were in a calmer frame of mind.

The pop singer was getting a reputation for being an influential person who understood the pressures that young people were under and was able to communicate with them. Leading Christians and campaigners saw that Cliff was a good person to have on their side, and soon they began to invite him to take an active part in their projects. This meant that Cliff was sometimes appointed to committees and commissions that wouldn't usually have anything to do with the show business world.

One of these was the Festival of Light, a campaign which hoped to bring back "light" to

Britain by cleaning up the nation's morals. It called for a return to traditional Christian values, such as the family and, as Cliff was keen to promote Christian morality, he agreed to become a member of the Festival's Council of Reference, a kind of steering committee.

The Festival of Light was supported by several other prominent people, including the journalist, Malcolm Muggeridge, and senior churchmen of various denominations, as well as ordinary members of the public. However, there were some people, including a number of committed Christians, who regarded the organisation as reactionary and hard-line, because of the way it condemned many aspects of life which people had begun to tolerate in recent years.

One of the main targets of the Festival of Light was homosexual practice. Its denunciation of homosexuality brought it into conflict with another pressure group, the Gay Liberation movement, which campaigned for equality for homosexuals and urged society to be tolerant towards them. At one of the early Festival of Light meetings which Cliff attended, at Westminster Central Hall in London, a number of Gay rights activists turned up to argue their case. With strongly held beliefs and emotions on both sides, the meeting was a potential battlefield but, ironically, when it came to blows, it was a little old lady who resorted to violence by hitting a burly opponent with her handbag!

In the early days, Cliff was wholly behind the Festival of Light, but he soon became less enthusiatic in his support. Technically, he remained on the Council of Reference, but he stopped playing an active role in the Festival's work because he was not altogether happy with the way it was handling its task. Cliff felt it was good to have taken a stand on morality, but in his view the movement had no clear idea of how to tackle society's problems on a more long-term basis.

Another committee which asked for Cliff's services was Lord Longford's commission on pornography. Cliff agreed to become a member because he thought it would give him the chance to put forward a Christian point of view. But he was never really a committee person – he tended to clam up in a roomful of experts. He also found committees frustrating because he saw everything in black and white, whereas his eminent colleagues seemed to reduce things to a murky shade of grey. He felt it was almost impossible for him as a Christian to discuss morality with people who didn't believe in the same moral absolutes that he did.

"It's so frustrating, Bill," said Cliff after another wasted meeting. "Pornography must surely be against the will of God, but I can't seem to get that across to these experts.''

''You need to argue the case in terms that they can understand,'' said Bill.

''But how? How can I argue with them? They just don't seem to believe in right and wrong. I don't think we even speak the same language.''

It was infuriating. Cliff knew what he believed but he just couldn't justify it to his fellow committee members, and that made him feel he was letting God down. Although he was now spending a lot of time presenting the case for Christianity, not just on committees, but also in meetings and in his books, he wasn't sure he was doing it as well as he could.

Cliff began to feel that he needed to learn more about his faith if he was to do a good job for the Lord. Apart from anything else, he seemed to be suffering from spiritual malnutrition because of all the Sundays that he spent speaking at other churches instead of being nourished at his own. If only he could go away and study and build up his spiritual resources! He was sure he could do a better job then.

But how would a busy pop star like him find time to do that? He had schedules and appointments and contracts to honour – he couldn't just go away whenever he felt like it. He thought it would do him good to go to college for a couple of months, but he knew that eight weeks is a long time in the cut-throat world of show business. Cliff explained his predicament to his manager, Peter Gormley, who could always be trusted to take his protégé's personal welfare into account.

"No problem, Cliff," smiled Peter. "If you feel you need time to go and study, I'll keep two months clear for you next year."

Cliff's idea was to spend his "sabbatical" at Oak Hill College, near Barnet, which trained people for the Church of England ministry. Most of the ordinands were on two- or three-year full-time courses, so it would have been difficult for Cliff simply to slot into the existing courses of lectures and seminars. Fortunately the college principal had arranged for Cliff to have a tailor-made series of private tutorials with various members of staff.

The young pop star couldn't believe his luck! Here was his chance to study the Bible at his own speed and with expert tuition. Maybe he could find out the answers to some of the questions that always had him stumped! But the value of Cliff's studies really became apparent after he said goodbye to the college staff and stepped back into his usual routine of Christian meetings.

"You must have learned something at that college after all," smiled David Winter at the end of one of Cliff's question and answer sessions. "I must say, your answers are becoming much more succinct."

Cliff felt it was his duty as a Christian to be able to explain his beliefs. But soon his mind was on something else that he regarded as a Christian necessity. He had slowly come to the conclusion that the baptism he received as an infant and the confirmation he received from the bishop after his conversion were not enough. He had read in the Bible that Jesus baptised his converts by immersing them in water, as a sign that their sins were being washed away. Cliff thought that the powerful symbolism of total immersion summed up his commitment to Jesus and his desire to be cleansed by Him.

As a new Christian, Cliff had initially attended Bill Latham's Anglican church in Finchley. He later changed to a Baptist Church, but that was not because of any strong views about Christian denominations. Cliff has always believed in being a Christian first, and an Anglican or a Baptist or a Methodist second. But now that he had moved away from his Finchley base to live in Surrey, it made sense to find another church nearer his new home. It just so happened that the minister of the nearby Guildford Baptist church, David Pawson, was an outstanding preacher and teacher, whom Cliff admired tremendously. Cliff felt he had found a church which would really inspire him and help him to grow as a Christian.

In a Baptist church, Christian parents do not have their children christened as infants. They dedicate them to the Lord, and wait for them to make their own Christian commitment when they are older, as the first Christians did in the New Testament. Candidates are baptised in a big tank of water in the church at a special service, with all the congregation there to watch and welcome their new members.

Cliff felt that this was closer to Jesus' example in the Bible than the Anglican system of infant baptism and adult confirmation. Because he had not been baptised after he became a Christian, he was beginning to feel that there was something wrong, that he had not done everything that God wanted him to do. He had an irritating niggle at the back of his mind and it refused to go away – not until he did something about it!

One very special day at Cliff's church, six hundred members had gathered to witness and celebrate the baptism of half a dozen Christians. To everyone's surprise, a seventh candidate got up from his seat in the congregation and joined the six newly-baptised members. It was Cliff. To prevent the press from turning up and transforming this solemn occasion into a media circus, he had made secret arrangements to be baptised.

He took off his jacket, carefully made his way down the steps into the tank, and clasped his arms across his chest. "Cliff, I baptise you in the name of the Father and of the Son and of the Holy Spirit," said the minister, plunging Cliff beneath the surface of the water.

This was it. Cliff was finally obeying Jesus' command to "Repent and be baptised." He was doing God's will, and it felt terrific. As Cliff righted himself in the pool, and the warm water trickled down his head and neck, he felt all the uncleanness in his life flow away, everything that had burdened him and made him less than human. It was a tremendous relief to have that weight of sin taken off his shoulders, and to feel like a bright new person.

The service lasted over two hours, but Cliff wanted it to go on forever. Now he knew deep down that Jesus had taken away his sins – he had always known it in his head, but now he felt it in his bones – and he just wanted to stay there and celebrate with all his fellow Christians. Until today, there had been something missing in his life, a little voice niggling away at the back of his head, telling him he wasn't complete as a Christian. But now he had peace of mind, and he was free to carry on with his Christian life.

One of Cliff's newer Christian projects that fired him with enthusiasm was a plan to create a

Christian Arts Centre, a place where Christians working professionally in the arts could meet and share their faith in a supportive atmosphere. The idea originally came from Nigel Goodwin, a Christian actor whom Cliff had met at St Paul's Church, Finchley back in the mid-sixties, in the days before Cliff's momentous appearance at the Billy Graham Crusade. Nigel had come to speak at the church's Youth Fellowship, and he continued the discussion over coffee at David Winter's home.

"You know what would be really great," enthused Nigel, "a place where people like you and me, who work in the arts, could go and meet. Wouldn't it be marvellous to be with Christians who understood the sort of work we do? Christians who aren't full of prejudices about the arts world?"

"You mean singers and actors?" asked Cliff.

"Yes, and musicians, and dancers, and painters, and broadcasters – people involved in any of the arts."

In those days it was not easy for an Evangelical Christian whose career was in the arts, because of the huge gulf that existed between the Church and the arts. Many Evangelicals believed that the arts world was sinful, and simply could not understand why a committed Christian would choose to work in such an unsavoury profession.

Cliff had come up against this judgemental attitude many times in the days since he made his faith public. His appearance at the Billy Graham Crusade triggered off a number of hostile letters from people who claimed to be Christians. The writer of one such letter put his point of view strongly: ''I would like to ask you how you reconcile the fact that you call yourself a Christian and also sing pop songs. Surely you are an enemy of the cross of Christ if you even consider that you have any dealings with this filthy world.''

However, this extreme reaction wasn't confined to a few isolated cranks, who happened to have a bee in their bonnet about pop music. Years later, another unpleasant incident showed the deep mistrust which existed for the arts in some Evangelical Christian circles. Cliff had gone with some Christian actor friends to take part in a congress on evangelism in Amsterdam, sponsored by the Billy Graham Organisation. The actors performed their piece of drama, but when it was Cliff's turn to sing, his fellow Christians from Norway walked out in protest.

There was clearly a need for some way to bridge the gulf that existed between the Church and the arts, so that Christian artists could have the same opportunities and encouragement to grow in the faith as Christians in other occupations. Cliff and Nigel thought that a Christian Arts Centre would be a good way to help them cope with hostility and integrate their faith and their work.

After Cliff and Nigel agreed upon their aim, they got together from time to time with a few other Christian artists to discuss the project, pray about it, and work towards realising it. However, it was to be a long time – six full years – before their vision for an Arts Centre became a reality. There was so much to do. They needed to find premises that would be suitably situated and not too expensive, appoint the right people to staff them, and raise money to pay for the necessary running costs.

After six years of searching for somewhere to meet, the group suddenly found themselves with not one, but two sets of premises. They had been looking for a property in central London, but it just so happened that an eight-bedroomed country house became available in Essex, and that triggered off the idea of a base in the country. "Battailles", with its eleven acres of grounds, stables, and squash courts seemed the perfect haven for overworked Christian artists to come to and relax on a weekend course or retreat. Cliff bought the house for the organisation, and the Arts Centre appointed a couple to look after it.

Around the same time, the Arts Centre Group also found a property in central London that would be suitable for a drop-in Arts Centre. Close to Kensington High Street, the building was very well situated and fortunately it was cheap to rent as well. After years of fruitless searching, the project was suddenly in action in both town and country.

"Buildings must be like buses," joked Cliff when he heard about the new London base that had been found, "you spend ages waiting for one, then two turn up at once!"

In July 1971, the project that Cliff and Nigel had prayed for, the Christian Arts Centre, eventually opened. It was a place where people from the arts, the media, and the entertainment world could come for lectures, debates, discussions, prayer and counselling. There they were free to be themselves and open up about their deepest feelings and beliefs in a relaxed atmosphere, without any fear of being ridiculed by the press or condemned by other Christians.

Unfortunately, the "Battailles" project turned out to be short-lived. The rambling house and its extensive grounds were too expensive for the Arts Centre Group to maintain, and had to be sold. A country retreat would have been pleasant, but perhaps the Group had been over-ambitious in taking it on at a time when they still had to get their London project off the ground.

Nevertheless, the London centre proved to be a great success. It later moved its premises to the

Waterloo area, to a building in Short Street, which was near the Old Vic and Young Vic Theatres. It is still thriving today, a living example of the fact that it is possible to be both a Christian and an artist.

Cliff has never felt that he can only put his Christian message across on platforms or in television interviews or gospel concerts. He seizes every available opportunity to explain the Christian faith to anyone who is willing to listen, in any setting, and is not deterred by his listeners' education or social standing.

The singer was once invited to a dinner party hosted by Billy Graham, when to his consternation he found that his fellow guests were to include two members of the Royal Family and a handful of top British politicians, including the former prime minister, Sir Alec Douglas-Home.

''What on earth am I going to talk about, Bill? What I know about politics would fit on the back of a postage stamp!''

''Don't worry, Cliff,'' his friend reassured him. ''I know precisely what you'll end up talking about – and it won't be politics!''

True enough, after dinner had ended, the conversation turned to religion, and Cliff was delighted to be able to converse with his eminent companions about the subject that was dearest to his heart. As soon as the guests began to talk about Christianity, Cliff was on home ground and there was no danger of him being lost for words. He may only have been brought up in a council house in Cheshunt, but he went home that evening knowing he had a message that even the rulers of the land needed to hear.

9.

WHO'S COUNTING?

1976 was a momentous year for Cliff, with the success of "I'm Nearly Famous", "Devil Woman" and "Miss You Nights", and his conquest of the American market, but the next few years were every bit as special. Cliff's succession of record-breaking achievements, anniversary celebrations, and accolades meant that he was never out of the public gaze for very long.

The year 1977, with Cliff's memorable trip to the TEAR Fund projects in Bangladesh, was an outstanding one for him for several other reasons. His numerous books on Christianity and the Bible were best-sellers all over the world, but it was his autobiography, *Which One's Cliff?*, which gave Cliff his opportunity to win a place in the *Guinness Book of Records*. During an hour-long signing session in a London department store, Selfridges, Cliff managed to autograph a record-breaking three hundred and thirty-three copies of the book. The previous record-holder had been the former

Prime Minister, Edward Heath, who only managed two hundred and thirty!

But that wasn't the only sort of record Cliff made that year! Cliff Richard's "Forty Golden Greats", a compilation album of some of his past hits, was another musical coup as it reached the top of the British hit parade. And congratulations were in order when the star was presented with a Music Therapy Silver Clef Award in recognition of his outstanding services to the music industry.

Now that Cliff had finally made an impression in the United States, he wanted to make sure that his new American admirers didn't forget him too quickly. Fortunately, he was invited to appear on American television on two popular programmes, "The Merve Griffin Show" and "The Mike Douglas Show". Meanwhile, back home, his British fans showed their loyalty to him by organising a National Cliff Week.

The following year, 1978, saw the first of a string of major anniversaries for Cliff – in this case, twenty years of Cliff and the Shadows! It was incredible how the years had flown. Could it really be that long since the lads signed their first professional contract and entertained the holidaymakers at Butlins? Little did they know that from these modest beginnings they would develop into world famous artists. Cliff and the Shadows had gone their separate ways in the intervening years, but this special anniversary was the perfect cue for a series of reunion concerts.

"You've had twenty good years, Cliff," said one reporter after a show. "That's a long time in show business. Will you be retiring now?"

"No," replied Cliff, amazed that anyone should think of such a thing. "I've no intention of retiring. I enjoy what I do and I'm just looking forward to the next five or six years."

The following year was well worth looking forward to, as Cliff continued to notch up a number of major successes. "We Don't Talk Any More", Cliff's first number one hit since 1968, sold a staggering five million copies and managed to reach number one position in several countries. And there was another anniversary to celebrate – twenty-one years with the record company, EMI. In time-honoured fashion, to mark Cliff's "coming of age", the company presented him with a gold replica of the key to the door, in this case, the door of EMI's main offices in London.

But Cliff had a real coming of age in 1980, as that was the year of his fortieth birthday. The former teenage singer was no longer "young" in years, but he still had more vitality than many people half his age and looked a great deal younger than his forty years. This birthday milestone had brought him to the forefront of public attention – not that he had ever been far from the public gaze in recent times!

The year got off to an unforgettable start with the announcement in the New Years Honours list that Cliff had been awarded an OBE for his services to music. The star had received countless accolades throughout his lengthy career, but none so prestigious as this.

That made it a problem. Cliff had mixed feelings about accepting such a major award. He felt deeply honoured that he had been chosen to receive an OBE but at the same time he wondered whether he ought to decline it politely. Here he was, a pop singer not yet turned forty, being given the sort of award that usually followed a lifetime of outstanding service to one's country.

Cliff had another reservation about it as well. Surely it would damage his credibility as a Christian if people thought he had only been chasing an award. He never wanted honours – his only aim was to serve God as well as he could – but would people believe that if he went ahead and accepted an OBE?

It was a difficult decision, but Cliff decided he'd better not do anything hasty. After all, he didn't want to cause the sort of offence that Beatle John Lennon had done when he returned his award to the Queen. There was another side to the honour too. If Cliff did accept the OBE it would be a great thrill for many of his supporters, both Christians and non-Christians, and they might be inspired by it.

Eventually Cliff decided that he would go ahead and accept the award, and be grateful that someone appreciated his work. Many people slog away at their job for a lifetime and never receive a word of gratitude or thanks, so Cliff knew how lucky he was to receive public recognition for the work he had done.

At last, the day came when the singer had to go to the Buckingham Palace to receive his award from the Queen in person.

Before he set off for the palace, Cliff took one last glance in the mirror to make sure he was smart enough to meet Her Majesty. "Well, then, Mamie," he asked, "how do I look?"

"Stunning," replied Bill's mother. "I like that red silk tie."

"It goes well with the black suit, doesn't it," agreed Cliff.

"I'm not so sure about those shoes though," frowned Mamie. "Wouldn't it look better with black ones?"

"No, I rather like them," said Cliff. "They're Italian leather, you know, cost me a bomb. I think they should go rather well with the red carpet at the Palace."

Buckingham Palace, with its ornate furnishings and historic chambers, was a fascinating place to visit, especially on a day like this when its halls were crammed with distinguished people from various walks of life. Their supporters were there too, beaming with pride for their loved ones' achievements. No one was more proud than Cliff's mum, who was brightening up the proceedings with her pink hat. Cliff scoured the audience for her, but it just so happened that pink was in fashion that year and Cliff didn't manage to pick her out from the sea of heads.

Inevitably there was a lot of hanging around before Cliff's turn arrived to collect his OBE, as there were over a hundred people who had to be presented with their Knighthoods first. Not that Cliff minded the wait! This was his chance to rub shoulders with lots of eminent people who normally moved in rather different circles from him – the civil service, medicine, and law, to name but a few. Cliff recognised a few faces from television or newspaper photographs, but many of them were just names on a list to him.

There was no chance of the Queen failing to recognise Cliff when it was his turn to go up and receive his award. The Queen smiled graciously, and shook Cliff's hand, but her double-edge compliment took him aback. She told the veteran pop star that she was particularly pleased to present him with his OBE as he had "been around rather a long time".

The ceremonial over, the band broke into a jaunty chorus of "Congratulations", never more appropriate than now, and at last Cliff felt able to relax and enjoy the splendid surroundings. It was a thrill to walk down the steps into the grounds and pose outside Buckingham Palace for a few special photographs for the family album. Then there were the many fans who had come from all over the country to crowd against the gates, in the hope that they would catch a glimpse of their hero on his big day. They deserved a wave and a smile.

After all the pomp and circumstance of the public presentation, Cliff opted to go for a quiet celebration with family and friends. He had arranged for them all to go to a private lunch at the Arts Centre Group near Waterloo. He was sure they would all want to know what the Queen had said to him – and wouldn't they hoot when he told them!

Cliff might have "been around rather a long time", but that didn't stop British viewers under sixteen from voting him Top Male Vocalist in a poll run by the Saturday Morning children's television programme, "Swop Shop". That was a thrill for Cliff, as there were many younger and more trendy stars for the teenagers to choose from. Maybe he wasn't past it after all!

Within four months the pop singer had added several other awards to his rapidly growing collection. There were the *TV Times* Award, awards from various national newspapers, and the BBC/*Daily Mirror* award for "Best Family Entertainer", to name but a few.

The next special event in Cliff's calendar was his fortieth birthday – but was it a day to celebrate or a day to dread? The way the media were carrying on, Cliff was beginning to wonder whether he should sign up for his pension book and walking stick. They had been talking about it for months, but Cliff couldn't imagine what all the fuss was about. To him, it was just another birthday – thirty-nine, forty, who's counting?

"Tell us, Cliff, what does it feel like to be forty?" the reporters clamoured when the big day finally arrived.

"Fine, thanks. No different from the thirtieth actually," replied Cliff obligingly. He would be glad when his birthday was over and people could start asking him more sensible questions.

The week before Cliff's birthday, cards and gifts had begun to flood in from admirers all over the world. There were sackfuls and sackfuls of mail every day, all crammed with love and good wishes. Cliff was amazed that so many people had taken the time and trouble to send him a token of their affection.

There were a lot of well-wishers who wanted to make sure that Cliff's fortieth would be a day to remember. Even though Cliff was working on his actual birthday, appearing in a concert at the Apollo Theatre in London, Cliff's fans turned the show into a special birthday celebration for him. As soon as he appeared on stage, the audience cheered him, and they wouldn't stop for nearly five minutes. They serenaded him with ''Happy Birthday'', not once, but several times throughout the evening's performance until their voices were hoarse. There was even a huge birthday cake, wheeled on in between songs by two of the sound and lighting engineers. Cliff was overwhelmed to discover that nearly every member of the audience had brought something for him, and all through the show they came and laid their gifts and cards and flowers at his feet.

It had been Cliff's intention to celebrate his birthday with his family and Bill and Mamie by having a private meal at the A.C.G. after the show. When he was ready to leave the theatre, the others went on ahead to the centre, leaving Bill and Cliff to follow in Cliff's car.

''Well, Cliff, did you enjoy the show?'' asked Bill, as they drove through the deserted streets to Waterloo.

"It was absolutely fantastic, Bill. The best birthday party I could have had."

"And now for a quiet dinner to round off the day."

"You bet. I'm looking forward to it. After all that excitement I think I could do with a bit of peace and quiet – especially at my advanced age!"

It didn't take long to get to their destination. It was only a short drive, and the London traffic was moving freely. There were few cars on the roads at that time of night and the only ones parked outside the A.C.G. belonged to Cliff's family.

"Well," thought Cliff as he stepped out of his car and walked the last few yards to the entrance, "what a day this has been! I don't think I've ever had a birthday quite like this."

To Cliff's surprise there was no trace of his mum, the girls, or Mamie in the centre. Surely they must have arrived by now? At last he spotted a familiar face in the hallway.

"Looking for your folks, Cliff? They went upstairs to look at the art exhibition until you arrived. Why don't you go through and make yourself comfortable and I'll let them know you're here?"

Cliff was ushered into an empty room, but to his astonishment it wasn't empty at all.

"Happy Birthday, Cliff", echoed dozens of familiar voices.

He couldn't believe it! In front of him were dozens of his closest friends from every walk of life – people from church, people from work, people who had helped and encouraged him throughout the years. There were some from Manchester and even the Channel Islands!

He turned to Bill, who was grinning like a Cheshire cat. "This is incredible!" said Cliff. "How on earth did you arrange all this without me knowing? I had no idea . . ."

"Elementary, my dear Cliff!"

All these friends he hadn't seen for such a long time! What a marvellous surprise! Suddenly Cliff's eyes clouded over and he felt a lump forming in his throat. "Thank you," he said. "Thank you – all of you – for coming here tonight. It's the best birthday present I could have wished for."

The next few hours seemed to rush by, as Cliff conversed with his many friends and enjoyed the rare luxury of having all the people he loved best together in the one room. The Arts Centre buzzed with excited chatter until the last guests staggered home at four in the morning.

"You know, that's what life's all about," said Cliff, as they drove home after the party, tired but contented. "Work is terrific, and money and fame are a nice bonus, but what really counts is having friends and relatives who love you. Nothing in the world is more important than that.''

The remarkable events of 1980 were a hard act to follow, but the next few years continued to bring Cliff enormous satisfaction. There was his *Daily Mirror* award for ''Best Male Singer'' in 1981, but his popularity wasn't confined to Britain. Cliff was also named ''Top International Male Singer'' by Germany's top-selling pop magazine.

There were major tours in America and Canada, and a couple of successful chart singles, ''Daddy's Home'' and ''Wired for Sound''. But perhaps the most flattering tribute Cliff received came from the BBC.

''You'll never guess what's happened, Mamie,'' said Cliff. ''The BBC have said they want to do some documentaries about my life. Four fifty-minute programmes! Would you believe it?''

''I certainly would,'' replied Bill's mother, not in the least surprised. ''After all, you've had one heck of a life!''

There were more foreign tours in 1982, this time to Hong Kong, Singapore, Thailand, Australia, New Zealand, Kenya, the USA and Europe, then it was time for Cliff to unpack his suitcases and celebrate his Silver Anniversary. Fan clubs all over the world were ecstatic that their hero had achieved twenty-five years in show business, twenty-five marvellous years at the top of his profession. It was an unparalleled record, and Cliff marked the occasion by playing six weeks of concerts at the Apollo Victoria Theatre in London, to the delight of his many supporters.

They were right to celebrate Cliff's anniversary. Cliff's career had been astonishing by any standards. It would be difficult to find another British pop singer who was so highly respected and so greatly loved. Hit records, awards, tours, television, films – Cliff had proved himself in all these fields. So what would the next twenty-five years hold for this phenomenal performer? What would Cliff's next professional challenge be?

10.

JUST IN TIME

"You'd be ideal for the part, Cliff," said Dave Clark. "It would be great if you could do it."

Dave used to be well known as the drummer of a band called the Dave Clark Five, but now he had turned his attention to writing a stage musical, *Time*. It was a science fiction rock musical in which the people of the planet Earth are threatened with extinction because of their continuing cruelty.

In the show a rock musician, Chris Wilder, has the task of pleading for the Earth's survival. For years Dave Clark had wanted Cliff, a real-life rock star, to play the part of Wilder, and now, for the second time, he was offering Cliff the chance to play the lead in a West End production of the musical. The first time he invited him to take on the role, two years ago, Cliff was keen to do it, but couldn't find a suitable stretch of free time in his busy working schedule. But this time it looked as if he might be able to reserve the fifteen months the project would demand.

Dave looked hopefully at Cliff. "How about it then?"

Cliff took a deep breath. It was a big commitment, but he really liked Dave's show and he was thrilled at the prospect of starring in a West End musical. "O.K., Dave," he smiled. "I'd be delighted to do it."

For over a year Cliff would be committed to performing the lead role in a stage musical – that meant seven or eight shows every single week. Every day except Sunday he would have to be at the theatre. It would certainly be a change from his varied lifestyle of the past twenty-odd years – a mixture of concerts, tours, recording sessions and television appearances, with no two days the same.

Fifteen months at the same theatre, playing the same role. How would he cope with the routine? The only regular job he remembered was at Atlas Lamps, but Cliff reckoned he would cope with his new life in the theatre. Surely starring at the Dominion theatre would be a lot more stimulating than pushing papers in a boring old office?

Not all Cliff's friends were sure that he was doing the right thing by agreeing to appear in *Time*. Some of them, the ones he called his "Job's comforters", warned him that his excursion into the theatre world was bound to end in disaster.

"You'll be bored out of your mind, Cliff. You're

used to seeing new people, new places every day. It'll drive you mad, fifteen months of doing the same thing every night.''

Cliff wasn't convinced. He was quite sure in his own mind that the time had come for him to go into the theatre, and this musical seemed the perfect opportunity. At last, after all these years, he could fulfil his ambition to star in a West End musical. His role in *Time* would enable him to do the three things he loved most in all the world – sing, dance, and act – so surely that wasn't too big a risk? His friends were right to point out the drawbacks. Fifteen months is a long time to commit yourself to one project, but doing *Time* wouldn't be a prison sentence. Not if he really liked the show.

That was the rub. When he first read the script Cliff thought the show was terrific. But now that he had had a chance to study it more carefully, he wasn't quite so whole-hearted about it as he had been. To be quite honest, he was beginning to feel uneasy about the project, but he wasn't sure why. On the face of it, *Time* was an excellent show, and it contained a powerful moral message about human responsibility.

Bill could tell that Cliff was fretting about the decision he had just made.

''What is it that's worrying you?'' he asked.

''There isn't anything obvious, Bill. I mean, it

doesn't have any swearing in it, or sex, or violence. And the story line is terribly ethical. I suppose what really bugs me is that it isn't Christian."

Bill raised an eyebrow. "Should it be?"

"I suppose not. It's just that with the story line being so moral, you begin to believe that the show is Christian, then it's disappointing to find some things in it that aren't."

"Such as?"

"Such as Jesus being referred to as a Time Lord. And Akesh being a bit like God, only he isn't really God. And the show making out that there's no such thing as death. Oh, and there are quite a lot of Bible quotations, but they're not always right."

"Well, does it matter? *Time* isn't supposed to be a Christian show, is it?"

"No, but I'm just worried that some people might get confused and think that it is. I wouldn't want anyone to get the wrong idea about Christianity because of it."

"If that's how you feel, then I think you should have a word with Dave Clark and hear what he has to say."

Cliff explained his misgivings to Dave Clark, the writer, and asked him if he'd be willing to make a few changes to the script. Cliff had to fight to put his case across, but eventually Dave agreed to alter some of the more contentious lines, such as the ones which referred specifically to Jesus. Cliff decided he'd be able to put up with Dave's amended script. He was still felt the show over-simplified the truth, but at least nobody would fall into the trap of thinking it was meant to be about Christianity. The show would go on, and Cliff would star in it.

By the time rehearsals began in January 1986, Cliff knew that everything possible was being done to create a breath-taking production. The designer, John Napier, had devised stunning sets for *Cats*, *Starlight Express*, and *Nicholas Nickleby*, and he planned an ambitious set for *Time*, using hi-tech lasers and lights. There was a model spaceship that would land on stage, and an amazing hologram to accompany the voice of Sir Laurence Olivier. The show was to be directed by Larry Fuller, a top American Director, who had worked with the legendary Barbra Streisand on *Funny Girl*, and on other hit shows such as *Sweeny Todd*, and *Evita*.

What Cliff didn't know was that the show would arouse considerable interest in Christianity and draw support from Christian groups, even though he felt it had religious shortcomings. Some of the ''Job's comforters'' among Cliff's friends had insisted that the show was theologically faulty and warned him that the churches would criticise him for taking part in such a controversial story. Cliff himself had been worried that the musical posed questions and dilemmas but didn't stop to answer all the problems thoroughly.

To his delight, this open-endedness turned out to be a strength instead of a weakness. Some members of the public who had seen the show wrote and told Cliff how it had affected them. *Time* had prompted them to think about their values and find their own answers to the dilemmas it raised.

Christians liked the show as well. Churches organised coach trips to see *Time*, clergy preached sermons on it, and one Christian magazine even printed discussion questions using the plot as a starting point. Although the show was never intended to promote Christian beliefs, it had got people thinking about the deeper questions of life, and so it was functioning as a useful piece of pre-evangelism.

Cliff's pessimistic friends were also wrong when they prophesied that Cliff wouldn't enjoy working in the theatre for such a long stretch. There were bad moments for Cliff, like the August Bank Holiday when he was involved in a car crash, and the sinus trouble which made it painful for him to sing high notes. But on the whole Cliff adored his fifteen months in the theatre. He threw himself into his new work with his usual enthusiasm, and found his new experience extremely enjoyable. His professionalism and desire to give the public his very best stood him in good stead in his new venture and impressed his colleagues. During his spell in *Time*, Cliff never missed a single performance, a remarkable achievement for any actor.

Time was popular with the churches, who found it thought-provoking, and with the general public, who made sure that the theatre was eighty-five per cent full for the whole of Cliff's run. Cliff himself told the press at his farewell performance, "You should write now that this is the greatest thing that has ever hit the theatre." Unfortunately, the critics were not so kind about the show. It came in for some harsh judgements, such as the *Sunday Times'* description of it as "an apocalyptic rave-in for affluent zombies". Cliff's acting ability was also called into question.

Cliff was astonished by the show's poor reviews. He considered *Time* to be entertaining, interesting, well staged, and full of marvellous rock music. The critics' hostile reaction was a mystery to him, and he made no secret of his disappointment. "To my dying day I don't think I'll ever understand why the show didn't receive a couple of accolades."

When Cliff agreed to appear in *Time*, he knew it would be extremely hard work, but he hadn't realised the physical and emotional effects that such a punishing schedule would have on him. He was certainly no stranger to hard work, but even so he found that every week when it came to Sunday, his day off, he felt completely drained. To begin with, he thought he might be going down with flu, but when he continued to feel the same way every single Sunday, he realised that this must simply be a side-effect of his exhausting theatre work. For six days every week he was giving a hundred per cent, and so it was not surprising that, by the time Sunday came, he was fit for nothing but bed.

The upshot of all this was that Cliff wasn't able to go to church for the whole of the period that he was appearing in *Time*. The star was so exhausted on Sundays that he simply didn't have the physical, mental and emotional reserves to get up and face a church full of people. As a public figure, Cliff has always found it difficult to go to church, because he can never blend into the background like an ordinary member of the congregation.

Cliff felt extremely guilty about missing church – he knew that some Christians would take a pretty dim view of his behaviour. To compensate, he spent extra time on Bible study, and he consoled himself with the thought that God would understand his predicament.

Needless to say, Cliff had to put most of his

usual Christian activities on hold while he was
working in the theatre. He didn't have the time
or energy to travel round giving talks to churches,
youth groups, or colleges. He was tied up at the
Dominion Theatre virtually every evening so there
was no opportunity to put on any gospel concerts
either.

"Isn't it a pity that you've had to stop your
Christian ministry for a year?" remarked one of
his acquaintances.

"That isn't how I see it," Cliff answered
quickly. "A Christian's ministry is more than the
activities he does. It's the way he lives his life.
While I'm in *Time*, that's my ministry –
performing in the show with all the commitment
and integrity that you'd expect of a Christian.
Doing the best job that I can, for God's sake."

Even though Cliff was unable to get out to
church services, the Church was able to come to
him, in the form of a group of Christians from the
Arts Centre Group who visited the Dominion
Theatre several times to hold Bible studies and
praise meetings. Cliff found these get-togethers
very encouraging, not least because they gave him
the chance to worship with other Christians from
the cast and crew of the show. Occasionally he
received visits from Christians outside show
business as well, such as two First Division
footballers who presented him with a tome called

The One Year Bible. That gift inspired Cliff to work his way through the entire Bible, something that he'd never had the courage to tackle before.

Cliff often went to the Arts Centre Group headquarters after the show, to have a meal and unwind, and to talk about his faith with other Christian actors and actresses. He enjoyed these discussions enormously. He felt they kept his feet on the ground and his mind on God, even though he was spending most of his time in the fantasy world of the theatre. It was reassuring to know that there were many other Christian actors and actresses appearing on stage every night, trying to combine their faith with the demands of their profession, just as he was doing. Now that he had sampled the rigours of theatre life, he had some idea of the pressures they were under. But, more importantly, Cliff knew that God loved him and would support him, no matter how frail or run-down he happened to feel.

In April 1986, not long after the show opened, Cliff found he was in special need of God's help and strength. Mamie Latham, Bill Latham's mother, was one of the mainstays of Cliff's life. The grand old lady had lived with Bill and Cliff for the past twenty years, and had shared many of the ups and downs of the pop star's life. She was a second mother to Cliff, and he loved her dearly.

Now, at the age of eighty-four, Mamie was in

hospital, critically ill. It was torture for Cliff to drag himself off to the theatre every night, knowing that Mamie would not be at home when he got back. He knew that she couldn't have long to live and he desperately wanted to spend more time with her at the hospital. He also wished he could give Bill more support but his demanding theatre schedule made this impossible.

On 24th April Cliff turned up at the Dominion Theatre as usual, to find that the stage computer system had broken down. Apparently it would take at least three days to fix, so the show had been cancelled.

"You can go home then, Cliff," he was told. "We won't be needing you."

But Cliff didn't go home. He made his way to the hospital to visit his beloved Mamie. He spent some time by her bedside then kissed her goodbye. Soon afterwards she was dead.

Mamie's death left a colossal gap in Cliff's life. Gone was the gracious lady who put up with his strange lifestyle and helped him with his problems. The house felt empty without her, even though Bill was still there.

Suddenly all the grief and pain that he had experienced at the death of his father came flooding back and threatened to overwhelm him once again. But this time Cliff knew he would be able to cope. He was older now, and stronger. He had Bill to share his grief with, dear old Bill, who missed Mamie even more than he did. But above all, he had his Christian faith, and that meant there was light even in the blackest night.

11.

CONGRATULATIONS!

Saturday 11th April 1987 marked another new chapter in Cliff's life, the end of his spell in the musical, *Time*. The pop singer had proved the sceptics wrong – he had adapted well to theatre life and enjoyed his period on the West End stage. It had been tough to begin with, when he felt drained by his demanding routine and the shock of Mamie's death, but he had won through.

Tonight, at the end of Cliff's last performance, Dave Clark and the cast were to thank Cliff publicly for all his hard work and bid him farewell. Soon, an American pop star, David Cassidy, would take over the starring role. But tonight belonged to Cliff and the spotlight was on him alone.

Dave Clark and the theatre management had done everything they could to provide Cliff with a magnificent send-off. There were speeches and goodbyes and votes of thanks, including a special tribute to Cliff from Dave Clark, who wrote the musical.

"It has been an experience to work with Cliff," he said, and explained that he had been very impressed with the way in which Cliff had coped with the demands of the theatre. It was a sign of Cliff's professionalism that he was always at the theatre two hours before the start of the performance and on stage five minutes before curtain up.

"You are a credit to our profession," declared Dave, as he presented Cliff with a memento of his many months in the show – a photograph showing the Dominion Theatre at night with the title of the show emblazoned across it in lights. It would remind Cliff of his excursion into the theatre world – as if he could ever forget!

As Cliff accepted his parting gift to ecstatic applause, he felt very emotional. He was pleased that he had taken part in *Time*, proud that he had taken on a new challenge and seen it through successfully. Some people had tried to dissuade him from this venture, convinced that he wouldn't be suited to the regular routine of live theatre, but he had loved every minute of his new life at the Dominion.

"I haven't had one boring moment", he told the audience, and he meant it. He had taken to the stage like a duck to water, and now that he had grown to love this strange and demanding, but wonderful, world of the theatre, how could he bear to leave it? He thought of all the things he would miss when he was no longer part of the show – the people from the cast and crew whom he had got to know so well, the familiar routine, the dressing room which he had made into a home from home, and, above all, the thrill of meeting a new group of people every night and transporting them into a magical world of make-believe.

He loved theatre life. And he loved the show as well, in spite of his initial misgivings about the story line, in spite of some cutting comments from the press. He praised the production warmly, and told any journalists who happened to be present that they should be recommending the show, not criticising it.

When all the public goodbyes had been said, the haunting strains of bagpipes filled the air as a piper in full Scottish dress came on stage to play the traditional farewell, ''Auld Lang Syne''. Cliff hoped that he wouldn't forget the friends he had made and the happy months he had spent at the Dominion. Perhaps some day he would have the chance to star in another musical?

Many of the audience had tears in their eyes by the time the performers slowly filed off stage, singing their last chorus of ''It's in Everyone of Us''. To resounding cries of ''We want Cliff'', the Dominion Theatre closed its curtains for the last time on its newest and brightest musical star.

Now it was time to look to the future, and for Cliff that meant resuming his international rock'n'roll career. But before that he was looking forward to a well-earned rest in Portugal!

After his break, Cliff slotted back into his busy schedule of recordings and rock concerts with amazing alacrity. Interrupting his pop career to work in the theatre had certainly not affected his popularity. Within four months he had reached the top ten with two new singles, ''My Pretty One'' and ''Some People'', and his aptly titled album, ''Always Guaranteed'', was proving very successful. The album earned Cliff a rare distinction, a Platinum Disk, for the sales in Denmark, and it was only the second time in the history of Denmark that such an award had been given.

In the second half of the year Cliff was on the road once again with a tour consisting of fifty performances in twelve European countries. But it was his concerts at the Birmingham National Exhibition Centre that were the best testimony to his enduring popularity. Cliff managed to fill the huge 11,600-seater Exhibition Centre for six consecutive nights, and was the first artist ever to achieve this feat.

However, it wasn't only work that occupied

Cliff's thoughts now that he was free of the heavy demands of the theatre. He had been a keen tennis player for many years, and at one time he had been in a relationship with the international tennis professional, Sue Barker. Cliff found tennis a wonderful way to unwind, and playing for two hours a day helped to keep him fit and trim.

It occurred to him that there must be lots of British youngsters who had the potential to be star tennis players, except that they weren't receiving the tuition and the encouragement that they needed to develop their talent. Cliff decided he would set up a scheme to give many children the chance to try out the game at special summer "fun days", free of charge, and provide special coaching for youngsters who showed particular promise.

The Cliff Richard "Search for a Star" scheme received sponsorship from the Mortgage Corporation, but a pro-celebrity tennis event was organised to raise public awareness and give the project's finances a welcome boost. The event, which has now become annual, was to take place in Brighton just before Christmas. For tennis-loving Cliff, a few games of tennis with some of his show biz colleagues and some willing professionals would be an ideal way to bring the year to an end.

"This is the life," thought Cliff as he gave the tennis ball a good, hard thwack and was rewarded with cheers from his spectators. "Here I am having a whale of a time and raising money for a good cause to boot!"

The crowd applauded wildly, loving every minute of the tournament. But no one was more delighted to be there than Cliff. On that chill December day, Cliff found it comforting to think that tennis courts all over the country might one day be swarming with excited youngsters having their first taste of the game that was so dear to his heart.

No sooner had Cliff hung up his tennis racket than it was time to pack again for another gruelling tour, this time of Australia and New Zealand. His tour of Australasia would occupy the first three months of 1988, and there were more European concerts planned for May.

"It's a good job I enjoy travelling," thought Cliff, as he set off on yet another long-haul flight. "I must have been to more countries in the world than just about anybody!"

Back on British soil after the tour, he was soon absorbed in another new project, devising and recording his new double album, "Private Collection", which was to be a compilation of his hits from the past ten years. There were a couple of religious projects in the pipeline as well. Cliff was to take part in the huge Christian rock festival, Greenbelt, and he was also due to launch his latest Christian book, *Single Minded*, which he had written with Bill Latham's help.

Single Minded was a biographical work which dealt with Cliff's more recent career, including the year he had just spent in *Time*. In *Single Minded*, Cliff discussed some of the personal questions he was frequently asked, including the hoary chestnut, "Why are you still single?", which was one reason for the book's title. "Single minded" was also a good description of the dedication which kept Cliff at the top of his profession but, most importantly, the title described Cliff's religious commitment. Now that he was a Christian, Cliff's mind was first and foremost on God.

Once Cliff had fulfilled his Christian engagements, it was time for him to tour the United Kingdom. To Cliff's amazement, the tickets for each of the forty-seven shows were completely sold out within seventy-two hours of them going on sale – over two hundred thousand tickets snapped up in a flash! Some fans had been so determined to see their hero that they queued all night to make sure they would get a ticket.

Cliff was over the moon at the end of the year when the "Private Collection" album and his new single, a Christmassy song called "Mistletoe and Wine", both reached number one. These chart successes brought Cliff's hectic year to a triumphant conclusion.

But before the year was out, Cliff was to compere an extra-special television show, the Christmas edition of BBC Television's "Songs of Praise". The programme gave viewers a chance to share in the Christmas celebrations of the Arts Centre Group, which was composed of Christians who worked in the entertainment world and the media. Cliff had helped to found the Centre back in 1971, and had supported it ever since. Like many of his fellow artists, he found the Arts Centre a marvellous place to unwind and chat about Christianity, and the building had also been the venue for some of his most memorable family celebrations. The "Songs of Praise" special attracted eleven and a half million viewers.

After another tour of New Zealand and Australia at the start of 1989, Cliff had his hands full collecting more prestigious awards. Congratulations seemed to be in order all year round these days! His fellow performers from the Variety Club of Great Britain presented him with one of their major awards, and this was soon followed by the BPI council ("Brits") award for outstanding musical achievement. Cliff and the Shadows made history when they became the only musicians ever to be awarded the Nordoff-Robbins Music Therapy Centre's Silver Clef for a second time, in recognition of the considerable financial support they had provided over the years. There was yet another *TV Times* award for Cliff, this time for Top Male Artist, and the magazine *Music Week* presented the singer with their 1988 Top Single award for "Mistletoe and Wine" as well as second prize in the Top Album category for "Private Collection". April brought Cliff a major accolade — a special Ivor Novello Award to celebrate the thirty years he had spent in the music business.

In May congratulations were again in order, and press cameras were clicking away as Cliff's latest record-breaking achievement hit the headlines. The singer had made history by becoming the only British artist ever to notch up a hundred single record releases. His new single, his hundredth, celebrated his thirty year career in show business and was appropriately entitled "The Best of Me". It was rapidly followed by another two chart singles, "I Just Don't Have the Heart" and "Lean on You", as well as an album, "Stronger", which sold a remarkable half million copies before it was even released.

There had been many successes to celebrate during the past couple of years, but the most important occasion was yet to come – the thirtieth anniversary of Cliff's musical career. He had spent thirty outstandingly successful years in the precarious world of show business. What would be a fitting way to celebrate such a remarkable achievement?

Concert promotor, Mel Bush, had the perfect solution.

"Wembley Stadium! Why don't we organise a concert for you at Wembley, Cliff?"

Cliff couldn't believe what he was hearing. "But that must hold over seventy thousand people!"

"Seventy-two thousand," answered Mel.

"Are you sure we can fill it?" asked Cliff. "I mean, the largest place I've ever played in Britain was the Birmingham NEC, and that only held eleven thousand."

"We'll fill it," said Mel. "Twice over. It'll be a sell-out."

Cliff still found it hard to believe that people would come and watch him in such vast numbers. Eventually he persuaded Mel that they ought to advertise only one concert to begin with. But when Cliff heard that the tickets had sold out in three days, he began to think that Mel might be right after all.

"Sold out, all seventy-two thousand, and we still had to turn away thousands of fans. I think we can go ahead with the second show, don't you?''

Cliff nodded, still finding these huge numbers mind-boggling. He just hoped everything would be all right. What if the weather was bad? What if it rained during the concert? What if . . .?

Soon there was no time to worry. The Wembley concerts would require complex organisation and lengthy preparations. Wembley Stadium was an awesome venue, and Cliff wanted his anniversary shows to be equally impressive. An army of burly craftsmen constructed a huge stage at one end of the stadium, then a hundred and twenty technicians set to work to make sure that the sound quality would be impeccable and the lighting spectacular. The show would require a hundred and fifty-six microphones, and twenty-four tons of sound equipment, not to mention ten miles of cable! Television crews would also have to set up all their paraphernalia, for ITV was planning to record the show and broadcast three special programmes, ''Cliff Richard – The Event'', at later dates. That would enable millions of Cliff Richard fans to share in the excitement of his spectacular celebration concert.

Meanwhile Cliff was selecting numbers for the show, and rehearsing routines with a dance group until every movement was perfect. There was work to be done with Cliff's supporting artists as well. The anniversary concert was a marvellous excuse for Cliff to get together with some of the musicians he had worked with many years ago, and some he had met more recently. Jet Harris would be taking part, and Tony Meehan, and the popular composers, Stock, Aitken, Waterman, who had provided Cliff with one of his recent chart successes. Cliff was also to sing with the American Kalin Twins, whom he had toured with in the fifties, when the Shadows' record, ''Move It'', had suddenly replaced the Kalin Twins' single at the top of the hit parade.

The audience had clamoured for Cliff at those early concerts, and it would be the same now. But when Cliff was making his debut back in 1959 and hitting the headlines for his smouldering looks and sexy pout, who would have guessed that he would still be at the top thirty years later?

On the night of the first Wembley concert, there was a marvellous atmosphere in the stadium. The audience were here to join in their hero's anniversary celebrations and enjoy a terrific evening's entertainment. Fortunately, Cliff's shows were not plagued by any of the problems that often accompany big rock concerts. There were no drugs, or vandalism, or fighting here, just a stadium full of orderly fans, intent on having a terrific evening. The police were amazed at how well the massive audience behaved, and said afterwards, ''The worst thing that happened was that they overfed our horses.''

That first evening there must have been some very frustrated ticket-holders, as a tube strike had played havoc with everyone's travel arrangements, and many fans were caught up in horrendous traffic jams on their way to Wembley. Some fans were two or three hours late in getting to the grounds, and missed part of the concert. But nobody allowed their frustration to taint the atmosphere of peace and good will inside the Stadium. Nothing was going to spoil Cliff's special evening. The audience listened and watched and cheered as Cliff regaled them with old favourites and some of his more recent hits.

By the end of the concert, darkness had fallen, but fans lit up the stadium with thousands of hand-held torches, which glittered like stars against the black of the night. As the closing song, ''From A Distance'', came to an end, Cliff looked out onto the galaxy of lights and, just for a moment, time stood still. He had been incredibly privileged throughout his life. He had been blessed with a supportive family, a wonderful career, and his religious faith. He had been given the gift of making music, to bring happiness to many, many people, and because of his success he had been able to help others. Yes, he had made a lot of people happy, but no one was happier than Cliff himself.

''I can't tell you what this has meant,'' he said to his fans, his voice heavy with emotion. ''I can just say thank you, all of you,'' and in his heart he thanked God for all the blessings he had enjoyed throughout his exceptionally happy life.

12.

STRONGER

It was 14th October 1990, and at last the press could ask the question which had been on their minds for most of the year.

"How does it feel to be fifty, Cliff?"

Ten years ago, Cliff had taken his fortieth birthday in his stride and couldn't understand why everyone was making such a fuss about it. But now that he had reached the age of fifty, he thought it was pretty remarkable that he was still singing and dancing, still holding his own in what many people regarded as a young person's profession.

"I'm half a century old, and to me that's fantastic," he told the assembled reporters. "It's going to be a bigger achievement for me than being forty. I'll be on my way to that telegram from the Queen."

"It's going to be a bigger achievement for me than being forty." It was a light-hearted remark, but behind it lay a deeper truth. Being fifty did make a difference, because the past ten years had enabled Cliff to develop and flourish, inwardly as well as outwardly. It was no coincidence that Cliff had used the title "Stronger" for a recent album and single, for the singer had become a much stronger person in many ways.

Professionally he had moved with the times and taken on new challenges, such as appearing on stage in the musical, *Time*. But in his more familiar role as a rock singer, he had proved to the music business that he was a force to be reckoned with. In terms of sheer volume, no other star could match the prodigious output of his long career. Cliff had now released well over a hundred singles, and spent more weeks in the British singles charts than any other pop singer. He rivalled the legendary Elvis Presley in the number of solo top ten hits he achieved.

But Cliff's most recent successes had shown that the veteran singer was not just living off his former glory. Cliff Richard could give any of the young up-and-coming stars a run for their money, as he demonstrated when he ousted Kylie Minogue and Jason Donovan from the top of the charts with "Mistletoe and Wine". In the past couple of years he had two Christmas number ones, and a couple of records at number three. His massive sell-out concerts at Birmingham and Wembley, extraordinary by any standards, testified that he was more popular with the British public than he had ever been, and his numerous foreign tours were proof of his worldwide appeal. It was clear that, professionally, Cliff had gone from strength to strength.

And physically, the fifty-year-old was extremely fit by anybody's standards. He kept lean and healthy by following a careful diet, supplemented by multivitamins, kelp, and Royal Jelly, while energetic dance routines and regular tennis had made him strong and supple. The professional dancers who worked with him on one of his recent tours of New Zealand and Australia were amazed at Cliff's stamina. Although they were only half his age, they found it difficult to keep up with him.

The passing years had enabled Cliff to mature as a person and come to terms with the advantages and disadvantages of his unusual lifestyle. For three decades the star had been under relentless pressure from the press to conform to their expectations. He had endured a constant barrage of questions about his personal life. "Why have you never married, Cliff?" "When are you going to settle down, Cliff?" But now at fifty he could point out honestly that he had already settled down in his own way, thank you very much. He was comfortable in his house in Surrey with its pool and tennis courts, and as for the pleasures of family life, he had his mother and sisters and ten young nieces and nephews.

Ever since he became a Christian, Cliff had experienced another constraint. He felt he needed to keep his religious sentiments separate from his rock'n'roll in case he alienated fans. Back in the sixties, the Church and the music business had seemed poles apart. Some church people argued that it was impossible to be a Christian and a rock singer, and in the music business some people maintained that Cliff's religious conversion would lose him fans. It's not surprising that for many years Cliff largely confined his religious music to gospel albums and concerts, reserving it for audiences who expected to hear about Christianity.

But now that Cliff had been a Christian rock singer for twenty-five years, he no longer had any doubts that rock music and Christianity could mix quite happily. He was confident enough by now to believe that his fans wouldn't desert him just because he included Christian songs in his commercial concerts. As he became more at ease with his dual identity, he began to feel more free to be himself. He risked mixing the sacred and the secular in albums and concerts, and was delighted to find that the combination worked. He had hated having to keep his religion in a separate compartment, and it was a relief not to have to do that any more.

Over the years the star's eyes had been opened to many of the world's problems – poverty, injustice, illness – and, to his credit, he had done something positive in response. He continued to support his first love, TEAR Fund, in its valuable work in the Third World, but he also added a number of other good causes to his list. He set up two funds of his own, the Cliff Richard Charitable Trust, which funds medical research and helps children and old people in Britain, and the Cliff Richard "Search for a Star" Scheme to promote tennis among British children. Cliff gave substantial support to the Nordoff-Robbins Music Therapy Centre; he sang with fellow stars as part of Band Aid's fund-raising efforts; and he adopted a mother and child whom he met on a visit to Haiti.

His Christian witness had grown stronger and bolder too. As a famous pop star Cliff has been given more opportunities to speak to the mass media than almost any other Christian in the history of the world. Through concerts, meetings, interviews and television appearances, he has been able to make his Christian message heard in millions of homes throughout the world. As his confidence increased, he found himself able to speak out about Christianity in secular concerts and appearances as well as in his Christian meetings.

Yes, Cliff was definitely stronger now. He had grown from a stage-struck teenager who wanted to be like Elvis into a mature man who was happy to be himself. He is an international rock star, but people remember him for his clean living, honesty and generosity. He committed his life to Christ a quarter of a century ago, but he has shown that he can stay the course. He sets himself the highest possible standards, and is content to offer God only his very best.

Not that Cliff would set himself up as a paragon of virtue. He would be the first to admit that he constantly makes mistakes and fails to match up to his own high standards. He knows as well as anybody that being a Christian is not an easy option, and he has spoken quite openly about how difficult he has found it to go to church or concentrate on prayer. "I try to present a positive image. But that doesn't mean I set myself up as a hero."

The story is not over yet. Hopefully, Cliff Richard will be entertaining the public for many years to come. His work schedule is as demanding as ever, and fifty-year-old Cliff is just as much in love with rock'n'roll as he was as a stage-struck teenager. When he was asked if he would be retiring now that he had reached his half-century, he replied firmly, "I'll never quit the music business. I'm still in love with the whole thing."

Cliff already looks set to add to his long list of professional successes. In November and December 1990 he broke another record by becoming the first performer ever to appear for fourteen consecutive dates at the Birmingham N.E.C. and to perform eighteen concerts at Wembley Arena. No doubt the future will hold more record-breaking achievements, more hits, more tours, more awards.

But there will probably be some surprises too, for Cliff is always adaptable, ever ready to rise to a new challenge. Perhaps this time he will try his hand at song-writing, or go back into films, or devise a new television series? Maybe he will decide to branch out into straight acting, or star in another stage musical? Who knows?

What is certain is that, whatever Cliff does in the future, his Christian faith will come shining through and sustain him in his work. Cliff Richard has had a remarkable musical career, which has brought him considerable joy and satisfaction, as well as immense fame and wealth. But there is no doubt at all where his heart really lies.

''Rock'n'roll doesn't mean a thing to me compared to what Jesus has to offer. And you know how much I love rock'n'roll!''